Crisis Management Planning for Schools

GARRY MCGIBONEY

Crisis Management Planning for Schools

Garry W. McGiboney, Ph.D.

EINSTAR PUBLISHING COMPANY

Published by EinStar Publishing Company

Library of Congress Control Number 2015897459

Print ISBN ISBN-13: 978-1530169511

Library ISBN-10:1530169518

First Edition by Garry McGiboney 2016

Crisis Management Planning for Schools

Published by EinStar Publishing Company

An imprint of the EinStar Publishing Group

Miami and New York

TABLE OF CONTENTS

CONTENTS   **PAGE**

Introduction

Purpose

Schools around the nation and the world face unprecedented challenges regarding threats to the safety of students, staff members, school schools, and the surrounding communities. Schools must be prepared for both internal and external threats – manmade, environmental, and situational. All crisis plans and management and execution of the plans must be done effectively and thoughtfully. The consequences for schools and the potential victims from a poorly developed crisis management plan or the lack of one can be severe and long-term. The collateral damage can destroy lives and reputations. The good news is the ample evidence and examples of how comprehensive crisis plans save lives and property and even thwart attacks on the safety of students and staff members at school. It is also important to remember that a safe school is an essential component of a positive school climate. If a school is working to change its culture by improving school climate, the job will not be complete if crisis planning is not an important element of the strategy.

The attention given to school violence sometimes diverts attention away from other possible incidents and actions that are dangerous, also. According to the CDC's School Associated Violent Death Study (2014), barely "one percent of all violent-related deaths of school-age children happen on school grounds or on the way to and from school or during a school event away from school. So the vast majority of students will never experience lethal violence at school."

There are other hazards more prevalent and are just as dangerous as violence in the school, such as fires and tornadoes. According to the United States Fire Administration (2011) there are on average over 4,000 school fires each year that result in from 75-90 injuries to students or staff members and cause over $66 million in property loss. Despite the danger of fires, only about 66 percent of schools have smoke alarms or established fire response protocols. Also, tornadoes cause an average of 70 fatalities and over 1,500 injuries each year in the United States, according to the National Weather Service. Additionally, there are very few school crisis plans that include specific roles of staff members, how the crisis plan will unfold or become operational, how the crisis plan can be adjusted during the event to be more effective, and how to organize a debriefing after the event to learn what needs to be changed in the crisis plan.

Too often school crisis plans do not include multiple threats to safety such as fire, weather, earthquakes, flooding, gunfire in the community, and many other threats. As was widely illustrated in 2009 during the H1N1 influenza pandemic very few schools include protocols and procedures for a pandemic or epidemic (Cauchemez, et.al, 2009). Despite the confusion and chaos during the 2009 influenza pandemic and even though CDC predicts the likelihood of another pandemic, probably from an influenza virus, only a few school have a crisis plan that includes pandemic or epidemic protocols (McGiboney, 2007).

Organization

This book was written to support and encourage the development and implementation of a comprehensive crisis management and prevention plan in schools and school districts. It contains protocols and procedures for a wide variety of crisis situations, including a comprehensive section on pandemic and epidemic planning and response. It is designed to be used as a general resource and as a training tool. It contains specific information, protocols aimed at operational functions, and it can be adapted to any type of school setting, including non-traditional school settings. In addition to being a crisis planning guide and training manual, the book is intended to be a quick reference resource, which makes the numerous checklists and specific language valuable as an immediate aid. The appendix also contains checklists and guidelines that can be used for planning, prevention and/or intervention assessments, debriefing exercises, notifications to the media, and parent and staff members information letters.

Crisis Management and Prevention and School Safety

A crisis can occur at any time and it is unlikely that any school will escape the necessity of responding to a significant crisis, ranging from severe weather to a manmade event. A crisis can impact a single school, the entire school district, or, as the September 11, 2001 terrorist attacks and the 2009 influenza pandemic demonstrated, the entire nation. For the purposes of this manual, "crisis" is defined as: *Any event that substantially endangers students, staff members, and/or the community or that creates a significant disruption of the school and/or community or that places students, staff members or the community in fear for their safety."*

All school staff members need to acknowledge that crisis management should include prevention planning and activities. That is why sections of this book include proactive, prevention suggestions, examples, and information. Leaders at the school district and leadership at the school level need to convey to all staff members that participating in the planning of crisis prevention and response and implementation of the crisis plan and their role in operating the crisis plan are all part of their job duties. Their failure to participate in, learn from, and act accordingly during a crisis could jeopardize their safety and the safety of students and other staff members.

Chapter One

Crisis Management Planning Considerations

"The secret of crisis management is not good versus bad; it's preventing the bad from getting worse.

-Andy Gillman

A comprehensive approach to crisis management places a strong emphasis on prevention. It should include strategies that establish communication procedures with local emergency management, a review school design and use of space, the development of student management policies, and the creation of plans for training of staff members. Crisis management planning anticipates potential problems and establishes a coordinated response to minimize threats to the safety of students and staff members and manages stress and disruption in the schools. A crisis management plan should also be developed with the goal to prevent a crisis from escalating. While it is not possible to anticipate all events, at the basic level there are elements that should be included in every crisis management plan:

1. Staff members participation in planning

2. Planning for a wide range of potential crisis events

3. Establishing a communication and information network within the school, school district, and with emergency responders

4. Establishing a coordinated response

5. Organizing and conducting debriefing sessions

Crisis management is a time-sensitive and focused intervention designed to identify, respond to and manage a crisis, restore order, restore equilibrium, and restore safety.

Foundation and Framework for Planning and Response

The chances of managing a crisis are increased if there are school district level policies and procedures that function within the framework of best crisis management and response practices and are tailored to conditions requiring a specific set of responses and resources. The development of policies and procedures that are appropriate and relevant for a crisis environment may need to deviate from traditional policy and procedure templates, because of the unique circumstances of crisis situations.

Benefits of Policies and Procedures for Crisis Management

Planning

Policies and procedures for crisis management and prevention provide benefits for students, parents, and the school district.

1. The procedures provide an organized, systematic method for preparing staff members and students for a crisis.

2. Staff members know under what circumstances and how to respond to an impending or possible crisis and an active crisis.

3. Staff members are trained on how to operate collaboratively within specified guidelines to make decisions and respond appropriately to stressful situations.

4. Staff members know under what circumstances and how to seek resources, report problems, make decisions, and work together to respond to rapidly evolving situations.

5. Parents, news media, and other members of the community are informed of the school district's actions and plans to be prepared in the event of a crisis situation, including how to respond to a crisis.

6. Interagency agreements, particularly with emergency responders and those agencies and entities with crisis response assets, foster stronger collaborative relationships and lead to a comprehensive community-wide response and management of a crisis.

7. No set of policies and procedures can prevent litigation; however, establishing policies and procedures based on sound practices and procedures provides some margin of protection against liability.

Framework for Crisis Plan Development

A comprehensive crisis management plan should be designed to effectively address a range of potential crises by including provisions for prevention and intervention and crisis response.

Prevention and Intervention Procedures

Prevention and intervention procedures provide an organized process for identifying, assessing, and intervening in a crisis that may include a potential or imminent threat or risk to students or staff members. These procedures are designed to prevent or reduce risk to the health, safety, and welfare of students and staff members and should include at least the following:

1. Training on severe weather identification and response

2. Training on staff members roles and responsibilities during a crisis

3. Training of students and staff members to recognize warning signs of risk

4. Immediate, mandatory reporting of concerns and events

5. Systematic assessment of threats

6. Expedited access to school and/or community resources for appropriate prevention and/or intervention

Crisis Response Procedures

Crisis response procedures should focus on situations which involve threats to students and staff members, such as natural disasters, school violence, accidents, and other situations. Such procedures should emphasize a coordinated response and are designed primarily to preserve and protect life and reduce the possibility of collateral threats to safety. Policies and practices should include the development of interagency agreements that specify channels of communication, types of services, and areas of responsibility. Such agreements typically are established with public safety (i.e., local or regional emergency management, police department, sheriff's office, fire department, emergency services), mental health agencies (both public and private), and public health. Sometimes it is necessary to establish agreements with businesses for resources and assets and other potential providers, such as care management organizations.

Procedures and practices should be problem-focused interventions designed to quickly and efficiently assess the crisis, disseminate accurate information, restore equilibrium, and support productive, appropriate responses for the following purposes:

1. To train leaders to recognize potential hazards and communicate and coordinate an appropriate response with their staff members

2. To protect life

3. To train students and staff members to recognize warning signs of risk

4. To encourage timely reporting of concerns/observations

5. To expedite access to school and/or community resources for appropriate prevention and intervention

6. To gather accurate information about potential or actual crisis events

7. To disseminate accurate information to staff members, students, parents, and, if appropriate, the media

8. To intervene directly with staff members and students most likely to be affected

9. To increase the available supportive services for students and staff members

10. To guide students and staff members to engage in productive, appropriate responses

11. To develop interagency agreements developed in advance of a crisis, specifying

    a) Channels of communication

    b) Types of services and areas of responsibility

    c) Agreements typically are established with emergency management agencies, public safety, mental health agencies, and public health agencies

Elements of Crisis Management

The elements of crisis management in schools should include the following:

1. **Policy and Leadership** – Policy provides both a foundation and a framework for action. The chances of effectively managing a crisis are increased with a school district level crisis plan and with individual school crisis plans which operate within the framework of the school district plan, but are tailored to the conditions and resources of the individual school. Leaders who understand and participate in the development of the crisis plan are necessary to ensure relevancy and effectiveness of the crisis plan as well as appropriate implementation of the crisis plan, including maintenance of preparedness and response. School district policies typically include the following elements:

   a. Definition of crisis

   b. Definition of prevention, intervention, and recovery

   c. Development of a district-wide crisis team and a plan with all elements of crisis planning and response

   d. A requirement that each school establish a crisis management team, including guidelines on the makeup of and the responsibility of the school crisis management team

   e. Development of a school site crisis management plan

   f. Specifications for issues to be addressed in the district-wide and school crisis management plans, include designation of chain of command, development of protocols for management of specific types of crises, coordination of communications, provisions for support services, staff members in-service training, and periodic review of the plan

g. Guidelines for working with local emergency management, public safety, mental health, public health and other agencies to coordinate a critical incident management plan

2. **Crisis Response Team** – A Crisis Response Team can be a highly effective organizational unit for dealing and preparing for a variety of crises. Such teams can operate at three levels: individual school school, school district office, and community. Well-functioning teams at each level provide a crisis plan and implementation network that can support action whenever crises arise.

3. **School District Office Crisis Management Plan** – A school district that is prepared for a wide variety of potential and active crises is in a good position to make appropriate and timely decisions if a crisis is imminent or during a crisis. The crisis plan should address strategies to gather information before, during and after a crisis. Additionally, the crisis plan should enumerate the responsibilities and roles of school district office staff members as part of the overall coordinated plan, including communication protocols, resources allocation protocols, and recovery protocols. It is important to include in the communication plans a method to communicate with every school in the school district, even if the crisis does not involve each school. A crisis will become known through the news media or through other sources and it is important for each school leader to understand the nature of the crisis in order to maintain control and preempt rumors in his or her school.

4. **School Crisis Management Plan** – A school that is prepared before a crisis occurs will be much more likely to deal with students and staff members effectively during and after a crisis. The crisis plan should be designed to result in a differentiated, coordinated response to crises such as severe weather, community disaster, death of a student or teacher, an in-school emergency, etc. The crisis plan should try to encompass as many possible crisis scenarios as possible. Too many times, crisis plans are too narrow and thereby focus only on a few possible crisis events.

5. **Critical Incident Management Plan** - A critical incident management plan focuses more narrowly on situations that involve imminent danger to life and limb and require a coordinated interagency response involving local emergency management, public safety, and public health resources.

6. **Training for Preparedness** – Preparation for and response to crises rely on people understanding policies and procedures and knowing what they are to do during a crisis and while preparing for an imminent crisis or possible crisis. These are best achieved through training. Maintaining preparedness is an ongoing process which involves debriefing following crises and following crisis response practices, periodic review, updating protocols, table-top (practice) exercises, and ongoing training.

7. **Communications** – Before, during, and after a crisis effective communication is essential within the school district, with parents and the community at large, and with the news media. Effective communication can speed the restoration of equilibrium and prevent uncontrolled and inaccurate rumors. Poor communication (i.e., lack of communication, incorrect information, etc.) can make a disruptive crisis situation much worse by prolonging the effects of the crisis and delaying the return to normalcy.

Example of School District Policies and Procedures

Crisis Management Plan

Definitions

1. "Crisis incidents" include but are not limited to situations involving natural disasters, fire, use of weapons/explosives, intruders, epidemic, pandemic, student violence, etc. Such incidents typically require an interagency response involving law enforcement, emergency services agencies, mental health, and public health. At the school level, the school principal has the authority to determine if an incident or event meets the definition of a crisis and when to convene the local school crisis management team and/or ask for assistance from the districtwide crisis management team or activate the crisis plan.

2. The individual school crisis management plan is a written plan with explicit intent to protect and sustain life, reduce emotional trauma, assist in emotional recovery from trauma, minimize personal injury and/or damage to the facility, stabilize the school environment and recognize potential hazards.

Crisis Management Team

District-wide and school crisis management teams should be established.

1. Membership: The crisis team should consist of an immediately accessible core group of staff members that have the knowledge and skills to plan for and act during any crisis. As needed, local emergency management, law enforcement, community mental health, public health, and public safety representatives should be asked to consult with the crisis team for planning and response needs. A roster of team members should be available at all times with updated communication information.

2. Purposes: The crisis management team should implement and adapt appropriate action from the crisis management plan to address potential, imminent, and active crisis and the specific circumstances of a crisis. Roles and responsibilities of team members and consultants should be established in the written crisis management plan.

Crisis Management Plan

Each crisis management plan should include provisions for preparation and planning, intervention and response, and post-emergency activities, including the establishment or designation of the following:

1. Develop explicit procedures for crisis prevention,

   intervention, and response

2. Develop crisis coordination and central command post, and a local school command post if the crisis is isolated to one school

3. Chain of command should be established

4. Identify at the school district office level or at the local school level a spokesperson to the media. This person is responsible for gathering and confirming all pertinent information about the crisis and for informing the school district superintendent prior to any media release. The spokesperson will also designate a media reception area when deemed appropriate.

5. A network of key communicators should be developed. It is the responsibility of key individuals to convey approved information to others within the school or school district. This network may include phone or text message trees to notify staff members of emergency preparations or incidents and special meetings which may occur before, during or after a crisis. It may also include staff members to support groups such as students, staff members, and parents.

6. Communication plan within the school district and communication with the community is essential. The best means of communication may depend on the type and nature of the crisis. However, a crisis plan should provide a method for communicating with parents and staff members as soon as possible. Well-informed representatives should be ready to communicate immediately. Prearranged communication modalities should be utilized to convey important information, such as through internal methods and, when appropriate, to the local news media to announce the circumstances of the crisis and other pertinent information, like closure of schools. To ensure accuracy and avoid rumors, information to students and staff members must come directly from internal memoranda or statements written specifically for that purpose and approved by the principal or school district office. When appropriate, information about a crisis is best given to students in class by a teacher so they can ask questions of a person they know. Questions from parents should also be addressed with accuracy while keeping in mind the FERPA restrictions on identifying students to a third party.

7. Arrangements should be made for support services and communications for school-based crises. Crisis management team should be designated to contact the school district office and to contact, as needed, other community resources such as mental health services, law enforcement, public safety and/or public health. The school district office should arrange for assistance, as needed, for additional school psychologists, school social workers, and guidance counselors even if nearby school districts need to be contacted to provide additional resources. School arrangements should include the designation of meeting spaces, provisions to request on-call services to meet unexpected demand, and provisions for long-term follow-up.

8. When a crisis has been contained and managed there should be plans on how to bring closure to the crisis

and begin the recovery process. This activity will vary depending on the crisis, but it is imperative to recognize officially the end of the crisis and the beginning of the recovery process.

9. Evaluation of the crisis plan response should start as soon as possible after the crisis has ended. Response to each crisis event should be reviewed in detail and evaluated.

Critical Incident Management Plan

1. A critical incident management plan should be developed in accordance with a Joint Memorandum of Understanding executed between the school district and leaders from law enforcement, public safety, public health, and mental health.

2. Specific school procedures should reflect utilization of an incident command center protocol and specify the key school-based procedures and methods of communication.

Crisis Management Training

The crisis management plan, including procedures for the identification of potential threats, should be reviewed annually with the school district office and local school staff members and shared with all staff members at the school district office and schools. Schools should be encouraged to provide additional in-service training on specific crisis related topics such as intruders, multiple injuries, community health emergencies, etc.

School Safety Mandates and Requirements

Many states have enacted legislation to address school safety and crisis management issues, and are requiring schools to develop crisis management procedures, often in the format of school safety plans. For example, in Georgia, the **Official Code of Georgia 20-2-1185 - School Safety Plans** requires every public school to develop a safe school plan based on crisis prevention and management.

> *Every public school shall prepare a school safety plan to help curb the growing incidence of violence in schools, to respond effectively to such incidents, and to provide a safe learning environment for Georgia's children, teachers, and other staff members. The plan shall address: natural disasters, hazardous materials or radiological accidents, acts of violence, and acts of terrorism. School safety plans shall be updated annually and submitted to the local emergency management agency. The Georgia Emergency Management Agency (GEMA) shall provide training and technical assistance to public school systems (crisis response team development, site surveys and safety audits, crisis management planning, exercise design, safe school planning, emergency operations planning, search and seizure, bomb threat management and model school safety plans.*

School districts should ensure that its crisis management plan meets the requirements of relevant state laws and local emergency management policies or ordinances.

Chapter Two

Leadership in Crisis Management

In crisis management, be quick with the facts and slow with the blame.

-Leonard Saffir

Leadership at the school district office level is critical to the successful management of and prevention of crises. School district staff members should support, participate in and encourage the development of crisis planning district-wide and in individual schools. School district office staff members should encourage prevention strategies, as well. When a crisis occurs, the school district office staff members must be prepared to assist in many areas while allowing school staff members to deal with the immediate needs of students, staff members, and parents.

Crisis Response Designations:

1. Senior Management

2. Public Relations/Media

3. Student Support Services

4. Facilities Services

5. Transportation

6. Technology/Information Services

7. Instruction

8. Finance

9. Human Resources

10. Operational Support

11. School Nurses

12. Public Safety

Roles and Responsibilities

The school district office functions should be delineated in the crisis planning process. In large school districts the roles in crisis planning and response may be more clearly defined because of the scope of responsibilities and logistical needs of several schools, centers, students, teachers, and resources. School district office staff members in small school districts will have multiple duties. Crisis leadership at the school level is equally important, because oftentimes critical decisions must be made quickly. For any size school district and school the roles and responsibilities in crisis planning are essential.

School District Level Leadership Functions

Senior Management (Superintendent and Central Management Staff members)

1. Directs all operations of the school district in the management of the crisis.

2. Gathers information from all aspects of the crisis for use in making appropriate decisions about the management of the crisis.

3. Assesses the immediate situation and assign tasks based on the overall needs for managing the crisis.

4. Stays in contact with the leaders of public health, emergency service agencies, law enforcement agencies working the emergency, as well as mental health and others as determined by the nature of the crisis.

5. Develops, reviews, and authorizes the release of information to the public and news media.

6. Actives the reunification sites in case students and staff members have to be evacuated from the school. Confirms that staff members are present at the reunification site along with law enforcement to maintain order, provide safety for students and staff members, and ensure that students and staff members are reunited with their families.

7. Keeps the local school board and other local officials informed of the status of the crisis, the response to the crisis, and the impact on schools and possibly the community.

8. Invites state and local officials to coordinate assistance and to gather information.

9. Alerts local hospitals to the possibility of casualties and reports immediately to the local hospital if students or adults are being sent to the hospitals for treatment. If more than one hospital is admitting students or adults, the leaders must coordinate the communication among those hospitals and the school district. Assigns and directs other division staff members to assist at those hospitals.

10. Coordinates communication with the hospital and parents.

11. If and when possible, meets and talks with the parents of students and spouses of staff members who have been impacted directly by the crisis.

12. Establishes and maintains lines of communication between the district and the crisis-site staff members. During an off-campus crisis lines of communications must be established for the involved school. Such lines of communication may also include the need for couriers if communication systems are inoperable or unavailable.

13. Communicates with all schools in the district during the crisis period.

14. Allocates assets and resources (persons and materials) to crisis sites for specific needs. This may include the assignment of staff members from other school or community sites such as community emergency shelters. If a crisis is imminent, assets and resources should be staged (put into position for quick allocation).

15. Identifies and when appropriate and necessary authorizes immediate purchase of outside services and materials needed for the management of crisis situations.

16.	Coordinates all services and personnel necessary to reopen schools.

17.	Coordinates debriefing sessions after the crisis.

Student Services (Support such as School Nurses, Counselors, etc.)

1.	Implements plan for the crisis and coordinates back-up student support personnel from other schools to assist, as needed.

2.	Maintains active file of support agencies within the community including the names of contact person(s) and a rapid communication protocol. The contact names should be periodically updated and verified, and the communication methods should be routinely tested.

3.	Creates letters (approved by school district office) to notify parents of continuing care that is available to students after the crisis. Available post-crisis care for students should include local support agencies, as well as school-based care.

4.	Develops information sheet for parents, teachers, and others. The information should include topics such as the impact of crises on students, signs of stress (including how to recognize post-traumatic stress disorder), how to talk to children about a crisis, how to regain emotional equilibrium, etc.

5.	Assists with planning and conducting parent/community meetings for information dissemination and post-event activities and participates in district website information development.

6.	Maintains follow-up communications and records on students and staff members that are referred to community-based support services, such as mental health centers, and coordinates well-check services when students and staff members return to school.

7.   Assists in the coordination of debriefings with staff members after a crisis.

8.   Makes recommendations to leadership regarding the restarting of school and schedule of activities for the crisis recovery phase.

Public Relations/Communications

(This critical function should be handled by someone who has had training on communications. If no one in the school district has communications training then at least two staff members should receive communication training as soon as possible.)

1.   Collects and disseminates information to the news media. The staff member should consider news media reporting deadlines, the need for information accuracy, and other issues related to the news media and accurate reporting of the crisis, as well as the school district's response to the crisis.

2.   Plans and coordinates press conferences - determines the location for the news media to gather, determines who will speak to the news media, and determines if news media questions will be answered.

3.   Quickly disseminates information to the news media and parents when students and staff members are evacuated to a reunification site.

4.   Creates and disseminates press releases (press releases should always be proofed by several staff members).

5.   Arranges interviews for the news media with key school and district staff members who are involved in the crisis or who act as spokespersons for the district.

6.   Acts as a liaison between the news media and school district staff members whose attention must be focused on the immediate problems of managing the crisis without constant interruptions.

7. Responds quickly to rumors through the dissemination of accurate information, and, when necessary, should quickly counter incorrect information or rumors – a timely response to rumors and incorrect information is critically important to control the crisis situation.

8. Organizes a network of key people within the community through which accurate information can be disseminated.

9. Respects FERPA requirements as well as the Freedom of Information Act and provides appropriate information to the news media based on those requirements.

10. Plans and coordinates the use of the district's website, cable television channel (if available) and social media to share and update information.

11. Coordinates development of information to be shared with school and district staff members during and after the crisis.

12. Establishes and maintains records of all communications during and after the crisis.

13. Coordinates a post-crisis debriefing on the communications component of the crisis management plan.

Facilities Services

1. Coordinates with transportation coordinator as needed.

2. Coordinates the crisis plan section that addresses imminent and actual power loss and includes the local power company providers in the planning process. Obtains and directs the placement of generators when power must be restored for a temporary period. Ensures that the power supplier is aware of the power disruption.

3. Coordinates the crisis plan section that addresses imminent and actual loss of water and sewer and includes the local water authority in the planning process. Coordinates and directs the acquisition and distribution of water when there is a disruption of water and sewer services. Ensures that the

water and sewer agency is aware of the disruption of services.

4.   Prepares and maintains accessible information for quick reference that includes school floor plans, architectural school floor plans, emergency shutdown systems schema, campus grounds maps, resources, material assets, etc.

5.   Communicates with community agencies as emergency facility services are needed.

6.   When appropriate and necessary, arranges for the delivery of outside services and materials needed for the management of the crisis.

7.   Plans and initiates arrangements for food and/or plan for the disruption of food services or supplies to schools.

8.   Participates in school district crisis debriefings.

9.   Coordinates the inspection of the school with local emergency and health authorities before a school is reopened.

Transportation

1.   Establishes the development of the section of the crisis plan that addresses transportation issues and response. Maintains and updates school district protocols for crisis transportation issues, including crisis-quick evacuations and alternative transportation routes.

2.   Develops and implements a transportation plan to get bus drivers to their buses when needed to reach schools for crisis-quick evacuations.

3.   Establishes and maintains plans for the crisis transport of students and staff members to predetermined alternate sites or schools for reunification.

4. Coordinates crisis transportation plans with local law enforcement personnel, as appropriate.

Technology/Information Services Role

1. Participates in the development of the crisis plan. Coordinates use of technology during a crisis.

2. Assists in establishment/maintenance of crisis communications networks.

3. Assists in obtaining needed student and staff member information and any facilities or resource data from the computer/data files.

4. Prepares and maintain a crisis access file that contains floor plans, telephone line locations, computer locations, and other communications equipment.

5. Establishes and maintains computer communication with the school district office and with other agency's communications systems.

6. Establishes and maintains laptops, notebook or other mobile computers with access to student and staff members database, digital floor plans, resources, transportation routes, etc.

7. With imminent and actual crisis, provides school district staff members with updates on the status of the technology systems.

Example of School District Crisis Communication Roster

(Some staff members will have multiple roles, and it highly recommended that these names and contact information be available from secured remote and mobile devices.)

Position/Role /Name /E-mail /Text Message/Work Phone /Fax /Home Phone/Cell Phone

1. Superintendent (or designee)

2. Assistant Superintendent

3. Facilities Liaison

4. Human Resources

5. Information Technology

6. Media Liaison

7. Community Relations

8. Safety /Security Liaison

9. Student Services

10. Superintendent

11. Transportation

12. Community or Agency Liaison

13. Other specialized

School Level Leadership Functions

Leadership of the school principal is crucial for effective crisis management. As the highest level executive in the school, the principal bears responsibility for decisions and activities. The following is a list of school leadership functions in preparing for crisis management leadership.

1. Review district-wide policies related to crisis management, including any interagency agreements. Gain a clear understanding of the channels of communication, lines of authority, and roles and responsibilities of both school district and community agency personnel.

2. Establish a school crisis team and work with them to develop a school crisis plan that includes basic principles of crisis response as well as sections that are tailored to the school's unique needs.

3. Establish a clear chain of command within the school. Clearly designate who is in charge in case of a crisis when the principal is away from the school.

4. Make a point of meeting, in advance of a crisis, with local law enforcement, emergency first responders, and public health officials who will respond to a crisis. Consult with them in developing the school's crisis plan and maintain the collaborative relationships.

5. Become thoroughly familiar with the school school and grounds, including the mechanical infrastructure, as well as the local community layout and assets as well as possible impediments, such as circumstances and features of the community, roads, topography that may disrupt a crisis evacuation of the school.

6. Ensure that all staff members understand the school's crisis management plan and particularly their specific responsibilities in the event of a crisis.

7. Prepare students to assume an appropriate role by enlisting their vigilance and conducting practice drills.

8. Assure parents and the community that the school has a crisis plan in place.

Example of School Level Crisis Communication Roster
(Some staff members will have multiple roles, and it highly recommended that these names and contact information be available from secured remote and mobile devices.)

Position /Name /E-mail /Text Message/Work Phone /Home Phone /Cell Phone

1. Principal
2. Assistant Principal*
3. Team Coordinator
4. Guidance Director**
5. School Secretary
6. School Psychologist
7. School Resource Officer
8. School Social Worker
9. School Nurse
10. Teacher/Counselor
11. Teacher/Counselor
12. Custodian /Facilities
13. Transportation
14. Food
15. Service
16. Others
17. * Designated back-up person in the absence of the Principal
18. ** Designated back-up person in the absence of the Crisis Response Team Coordinator.

Chapter Three

Establishing a Crisis Response Team

"I violated the Noah Rule: predicting rain doesn't count; school the

arks does."

-Warren Buffett

A crisis response team can be a highly effective organizational unit for dealing with a variety of crises such as accidents, intruders, suicides, incidents of violence, weather emergencies, etc. Crisis response teams in a school district can operate at three levels: (1) individual school, (2) school district, and (3) community. Well-functioning crisis response teams at each level provide a network capable of a comprehensive, coordinated response and recovery.

School District Crisis Response Team

In addition to individual school crisis response teams, the crisis network should include a crisis response team at the district school district office level. This team may include the district superintendent or designee and senior administrators in key school division areas of operation. The school district office crisis team consults with emergency management, law enforcement, emergency responders, mental health, public utility, and public health officials and takes the lead in developing and maintaining interagency memoranda of understanding defining interagency responses to crises. The school district office crisis network would typically have responsibility for the following:

1. Issuing critical communications and decisions

2. Overseeing and coordinating the school level teams

3. Authorizing resources for areas where they are most needed. As an example, providing more counselors to a school whose staff members may be overburdened in dealing with a crisis

4. Collecting and disseminating educational materials to schools for training crisis team members and faculty

5. Establishing a central library of materials on severe weather, sheltering, violence, suicide, and other crisis management issues for use by faculty, staff members, and students.

6. Conducting mock crisis events to practice and test the crisis management procedures

7. Preparing and maintaining information that contains communications protocols, floor plans, telephone line locations, computer locations, and other facilities essentials

8. Evaluating responses to crises

9. Establishing a community support team and encouraging input and support from its members

School Level Crisis Response Team

The school level crisis response team can be led by the principal, with an alternate leader designated to assume the leadership role in the principal's absence. In addition to teachers, the team may include guidance counselor(s), school nurse, school psychologist and/or school social worker, school secretary, and custodian. School resource officers should also serve on school crisis response teams. When school resource officers are assigned to a school, they should be consulted in the development of the school's crisis management plan and involved in responses to any crisis, especially those crises involving a violation of law or threats to the safety of students and staff members. The school nurse should take a lead role during a public health crisis. The school level crisis response team typically has responsibility for the following:

1. Establishing a written protocol for dealing with crises

2. Establishing a systematic approach for identifying, referring, and addressing a crisis (and isolating students who may pose a risk or who are at risk)

3. Orienting staff members to procedures and training to fulfill designated roles, including conducting table-tip simulations and practice drills

4. Providing information to students, staff members, and community on crisis management referral procedures

5. Providing assistance during a crisis in accordance with designated roles and providing follow-up activities

6. Conducting debriefing at the conclusion of each crisis episode to critique the effectiveness of the school's crisis management plan

7. Conducting periodic reviews and updating of the crisis management plan and conducting related updated staff members training

Duties of Members of the School Crisis Response Team

The **Principal** coordinates and supervises crisis management activities at the school. Duties include:

1. Continuity of administration

2. Development of a comprehensive school emergency management program

3. Designation and training of a school crisis management team

4. Designation and training of teachers on roles and responsibilities during a crisis

5. Designation of a command post (may be changed by responsible county public safety officials)

6. Monitor developing situations (i.e., weather conditions, an epidemic, incidents in the community that may impact the school, etc.)

7. Implement procedures and measures to control access to school.

8. Communicate with district office, law enforcement, public health, etc. during a crisis

9. Coordinate use of school as public shelter for major emergencies occurring in the area

Teachers are responsible for implementing appropriate procedures to protect students. These responsibilities include:

1. Evacuation - Direct and supervise students in route to pre-designated safe areas within the school or to an off-site evacuation shelter.

2. Classroom lockdown – Conduct classroom lockdown procedures in accordance with established procedures.

3. Student accounting - Verify the location and status of students. Report to the principal or designee on the condition of any student who needs additional assistance.

4. Student assembly/holding areas - Maintain order while in student assembly/holding areas to facilitate orderly student accounting and release or transport.

5. Establish a partner system to pair teachers and classes so that some teachers can assist with other tasks such as first aid, search and rescue, or community relations.

6. Remain with assigned students throughout the duration of the emergency, unless otherwise assigned through a partner system or until every student has been released through the official student release process.

Assistant Principal - Tasks related to student accounting and student release.

1. Follows procedures for assessing and reporting status of students in a crisis or any event that results in evacuation or relocation of students.

2. Provides instruction and practice to all teachers and staff members in the student assessment and reporting process.

3. Follows procedures for communication with teachers and other school staff members during a crisis.

4. During a crisis - receives reports from all teachers on the condition and location of every student, when appropriate.

5. Assigns persons to investigate reports of any students missing, injured or ill, or otherwise not in compliance with student accounting reports.

6. Implements student release procedures.

Maintenance Head - Maintenance staff members are familiar with the operations and infrastructure of the school and are responsible for the stabilization of the school, controlling access, and securing the school facilities:

1. Inventory all hazardous materials, portable and fixed equipment, and utility lines in or near the school.

2. Follow procedures for isolating hazardous areas.

3. In a crisis, survey any damage and structural stability of schools and utilities and report to the principal.

4. Search the sections of the school for students or staff members that may be confined, injured, sick.

5. Implement school access control measures.

6. Secure student evacuation sites.

7.   Assist local officials in damage assessment.

8.   Assist administrators in recovery procedures.

Elements of an Effective Crisis Response Team

It is critically important for members of the Crisis Response Team to work together. Individuals that do not trust each other will not be effective during a crisis and in fact could jeopardize important aspects of the response to a crisis. Members of the Crisis Response Team should process:

1. Professional maturity and leadership skills

2. A respectful and calm demeanor during difficult times

3. A respect for details, chain of command, and organization

4. A willingness to participate in the planning, implementation, and response stages of a crisis

5. Familiarity with the climate and nature of the school and its students, staff members, and the community

6. Willingness to problem-solve cooperatively and quickly, as needed

7. An ability to anticipate and recognize multiple problems and possible consequences

8. An ability to think clearly under stress

9. Strong communication, problem-solving, and conflict resolution skills

10. A devotion to the Crisis Management Plan and willingness to provide constructive criticism

Elements of a Dysfunctional Crisis Response Team

A dysfunctional Crisis Response Team can be easily recognized, but unfortunately it is usually after the response was inappropriate, inadequate, or a complete failure. Therefore, it is important for leaders to take note of elements that indicate that a Crisis Response Team is dysfunctional.

1. No organized, functional crisis plan has been developed that includes all elements of an appropriate response or does not include clear delineation of Crisis Response Team member roles and responsibilities

2. Team members are inflexible and didactic

3. The crisis plan is outdated

4. Team member roles and responsibilities are unclear

5. Leadership of the team has not been clarified

6. No clearly delineated chain of command has been established

7. Team members speak to the news media without a unified voice

8. Team members respond to a crisis independent of the crisis plan

9. Team members are involved in protecting their own "turf"

10. Team members participate in spreading rumors or unconfirmed potentially inflammatory information

11. Team members share confidential information to third parties

12. Team members withhold important information from colleagues

Community Crisis Response Support Network

The school district crisis network should include community agencies and organizations such as emergency management, mental health, public safety, public health, public utilities, and social services that can be instrumental in responding to a crisis and restoring equilibrium following crisis events. School districts should maintain regular contact with community agencies and organizations in the community support network and invite them to participate in meetings with school and school district office crisis management teams.

Chapter Four

Key Elements in Establishing a Crisis Plan

A good plan implemented today is better than a perfect
plan implemented tomorrow.
-General George Patton

As referenced in previous chapters, school districts and schools that are prepared before a crisis occurs will be much more likely to deal with disruption more effectively. Early chapters pointed out the various roles of leaders and other staff members in planning for a crisis and during a crisis.

Managing the Details

Moving into more detail in setting up a crisis management plan, the following activities should be considered.

1. Decide who will be in charge during a crisis.

A crucial first step in crisis management planning is to decide who will be in charge during a crisis. One person should be designated to provide leadership during crisis situations, to organize activities, and to disseminate information. Usually the person in charge at the district level is the superintendent, or his/her designee, and at the school level it should be the principal or assistant principal. A substitute should be identified in the event that the designated person is unavailable at the time of the crisis. It is extremely important that all staff members understand the lines of authority during a crisis.

2. Establish the Crisis Response Team.

A second important step is to recruit members for the Crisis Response Team. Typically at the district level, the Crisis Response Team is the superintendent's school district office staff members, while at the school level the Crisis Response Team consists of an administrator, nurse, psychologist, school social worker, teachers, counselors, and others with skills appropriate to the tasks to be performed, including school resource officers, when available. Sometimes forgotten, but important in crises, at the school level are the secretary/office manager, the head custodian, and bus drivers.

Most, if not all, of the team members must be present in the school full-time (or available and able to respond immediately to the school's needs). Some school districts have assigned bus drivers to full-time duties in schools, such as paraprofessionals, so that a bus driver and bus will be available at all times should a crisis evacuation occur.

3. Develop clear and consistent policies and procedures.

It is absolutely critical to develop procedures that provide all staff members with clear guidelines for tasks and responsibilities during crises, which also ensures that all staff members will respond consistently in each situation. This applies to each and every staff member in the school. There should also be a quick reference sheet for the part-time or itinerant employees designating the roles during a crisis situation.

4. Provide training for the Crisis Response Team.

Training for school staff members, such as from FEMA, local emergency management, fire services, and public safety is essential. Also, local staff members such as school resources officers, school psychologists, school nurses, etc. can provide training for the crisis response team.

5. Establish a media liaison and identify suitable facilities where reporters can work and news conferences can be held.

Many school districts have a community or public relations spokesperson that receives all media requests and establishes procedures for responding to the media in times of crisis. This important component was specified in a previous chapter, but there may be a time when someone at a school has to assume this role. A person designated for this role should receive training from the school district's chief information officer (CIO) or from other agency CIO's who have experience communicating with the news media and the public in crisis situations.

6. Designated Command Post and Staging Areas

First responders involved in several of the recent school crisis situations recommend that schools and first responders plan for three distinct staging areas, in addition to the Command Post for the

Incident Command Officer. Among other things, separate staging areas will prevent the press from converging upon parents or parents from converging upon police. The staging areas are very important for safety and crowd control. The areas should be:

1. A **First Responders Staging Area** for law enforcement and emergency personnel

2. A **Media Staging Area** away from the school, at a location that can accommodate a large number of vehicles

3. A **Parent Staging Area** located away from the Command Post, where parents can reunite with their children

Maps of all command posts, listing each corresponding phone number, should be included in the Crisis Response Box.

7. Establish a working relationship with community mental health, emergency management, public health, public safety, and other resource groups.

To facilitate quick and collaborative responses, strong relationships with community agencies must be established prior to a crisis. As referenced previously, the development of a crisis management plan should include community agencies, but that is not enough. It is important to build a relationship with key personnel in the community agency. This is done through frequent contact and communications, such as inviting staff members from the community agencies to visit the schools and participate in school activities on a regular basis. In a crisis, knowing the people involved in the crisis gives it a face and a name, which can be critically important during difficult times.

8. Set up a communications network.

Critical information needs to be communicated as quickly as possible to those in need. The network should utilize multiple methods of communications. The importance of accurate information cannot be emphasized enough. Also, communication devices are constantly changing, some of which have not been fully tested in a crisis, such as during a large scale power grid failure. Some school districts have through grants and through collaboration with local emergency management agencies purchased satellite phones for use when all other methods of communication fail. Satellite phone are expensive and are expensive to use, but they be worth the investment considering the conditions and circumstances of some schools and school districts.

9. Develop a plan for physical space management.

In a crisis a district office or school may not be able to accommodate the influx of emergency staff members, parents and news media. Crisis management planning should anticipate the potential space needs and designate space for media, public safety operations, public health, parents, and others. The physical plant will dictate choices; however, it is wise to take into account access to telephones, water, restrooms, food and drink. Staff members who direct people and supervise these areas need to be identified in advance and trained.

10. Develop necessary forms and information sheets.

Develop record-keeping forms to assist in the management of crisis situations. Some materials may need to be translated for families into languages appropriate for the school community. Also, accurate and clear record-keeping is essential for resource identification, resource restoration, and possible resource compensation. Too often during the turmoil of a crisis no records, logs, notes, invoices or other types of records are kept. The lack of documentation creates difficult situations for school districts with insurance companies and with claims to FEMA. An example of this is the horrendous damage to people and property caused by Hurricane Katrina. Many school districts used and in some places exceeded all of their local funding reserves trying to cope with the destruction of the massive storm while counting on reimbursement from FEMA or utilizing FEMA funds during the aftermath of the storm. However, due to poor recordkeeping many of those school districts either did not receive compensation for their loss or were required to pay back FEMA for the crisis funds they used during and after the crisis.

11. Develop a plan for emergency coverage of classes.

Teachers who will play significant roles in a crisis response need to be assured that their classrooms will be covered when they are called from the classroom to assist in the crisis. The use of part-time staff members, itinerant staff members, and regular volunteers as possible sources of assistance in classroom coverage should be included in the crisis management plan.

12. Establish a system of codes to alert staff members.

Establish a system of codes to alert district office staff members and the same for school staff members as to the nature of a crisis without unduly alarming the rest of the school while gearing up for a crisis response. This is part of the effort and plan to avoid panic between and among students and staff members. The plan should consider the possibility that a crisis can occur rapidly and escalate without warning, which means that a crisis alarm system should be developed that every staff members member is aware of and that can be activated quickly and efficiently.

13. Develop a collection of readings.

It is important for the school district's media services to develop a bibliography of books or web-based resources pertinent to crisis planning, crisis staging, and crisis situations for central office staff members, school staff members, and auxiliary staff members. Such resources are valuable in assisting the school community to achieve a positive attitude about crisis planning, crisis response, and resolution and recovery.

14. Have school attorney review crisis response procedures and forms.

School districts and schools should adjust crisis planning components to comply with any liability concerns, based on recommendations of legal counsel. This should include procedures for documenting crisis activities and decision making. While this can be a sensitive matter, there are times when an administrator has to make decisions without fear of litigation, because of the urgency of the crisis. A leader cannot be hampered or paralyzed from making decisions in potentially life or death situations because of legal concerns.

15. Conduct practice "crisis alert" sessions with staff members and students.

Prepare staff members for their responsibilities in a real crisis. Practice several types of scenarios, but the most frequent and most likely to occur would include severe weather events, evacuations and lockdowns. These practices should train students and staff members on what to expect and what to do. This greatly reduces the likelihood of panic during a crisis. Through table-top simulations and other practice sessions, staff members can become more proficient in responding to a variety of crises and it gives them the opportunity to contribute to the plan and to ask questions. It is best to avoid sensationalized simulations, particularly any activities involving students.

16. Conduct training in the school crisis response procedures at least annually and make it part of any new employee orientation.

Training in crisis response procedures is needed at least annually for staff members, with practices more frequent. Crisis response procedures should be part of new employee and volunteer orientations. Depending on unique situations or conditions at schools, more or specific in-service training sessions on crisis-related topics may be necessary.

Assessing Needs and Assigning Tasks

Crisis response teams should identify needs and match them with available resources. As a starting point, it is important to:

Identify Needs:

1. Areas of responsibility and tasks requiring attention in a crisis – this provides an opportunity to identify any unique needs in the school, such as how to evacuate students in wheelchairs or other students that are medically fragile

2. Physical space needs – this provides an opportunity to consider any unique structural or other physical features of the school that may offer assistance or create obstacles, such as an unused hallway that could allow a quick exit or a four way hall intersection that could impede movement of students if they enter the same intersection at the same time.

3. Communication needs – this provides an opportunity to discuss the most effective means of communications, such as identifying parts of the school that are "dead zones" for cellphone or walkie-talkie usage.

Identify Resources

1. Staff members skills, particularly in responding to crises – this provides an opportunity to identify and discuss staff members member's training, previous careers, and set of skills. Some staff members do not think their skills, experience, hobbies, or training would be useful during a crisis, but they should all be discussed to discern what skills could be utilized.

2. Physical space availability – this provides an opportunity to identify space resources, such as command center space, potential off-campus sites such as other schools, community centers, and churches, storage space for sheltering-in.

3. Communications capabilities in the school – this provides an opportunity to identify possible sources of communication, such as how many staff members have cell phones, are walkie-talkies distributed evenly or

strategically throughout the school, could computers like tablets and notebooks be used for crisis communications, etc.

Match Needs and Resources

1. Assign responsibilities for specific activities and tasks; designate back-up staff members in the event of absences – this provides an opportunity to make sure the staff members given specific assignments are capable of performing the assignments. This discussion is critically important to avoid random assignments of critical duties to staff members who are not able or do not have the personality makeup or the skills to handle certain types of situations. It is unfair to put staff members in that predicament.

2. Identify physical spaces for specific types of activities and assign staff members to direct students and staff members to the appropriate space with supervision. This provides an opportunity to discuss the potential problems inherent in moving large numbers of students and staff members under stressful conditions. Moving people quickly, efficiently, and safely is very difficult during a crisis and should never be taken for granted. An unsupervised, unplanned movement of students and staff members can create a hazardous situation.

3. Develop a communications plan with back-up strategies – this provides an opportunity to discuss communication failures and how to create and implement backup communication plans, such as the strategic placement of bullhorns throughout the school in case other communications devices or methods fail.

Example of School Staff Members Inventory of Skills and

Experience

Check any of the following in which you have expertise or training:

Crisis Response Skills

1. First aid – name and room location:

2. Logistics – name and room location:

3. Communications – name and room location:

4. Fire Safety / Firefighting – name and room location:

5. CPR – name and room location:

6. Search & Rescue – name and room location:

7. EMT – name and room location:

8. Critical Incident Stress Debriefing – name and room location:

9. Law Enforcement – name and room location:

10. Post-traumatic Stress Training – name and room location:

11. Other (Please specify) _____ – name and room location:

(Using information gathered in the inventory above, lists such as the one below can be developed for quick reference based on needs during a crisis)

Staff members with Medical Care Skills

1. Name:

2. Location:

3. Notification Method:

4.   Training/Certification:

Staff members with Communication Devices

1.   Name:

2.   Location:

3.   Notification Method:

4.   Type of device and contact information:

Bi/Multi-Lingual Staff members

1.   Name:

2.   Location:

3.   Notification Method

4.   Languages:

Staff members with Sign Language Skills

1.   Name:

2.   Location:

3.   Notification Method:

Students Who May Need Special Assistance in a Crisis

1.   Name:

2.   Location (schedule of all classes):

3.   Description of Assistance Needed:

4.   Staff members Member Assigned to Assist Student:

5. Location of Staff members Member Assigned to Assist

    Student:

Staff members Who May Need Special Assistance in a Crisis

1. Name:

2. Location (schedule of all classes):

3. Description of Assistance Needed:

4. Staff members Member Assigned to Assist Staff members

    Member:

5. Location of Staff members Member Assigned to Assist

    Staff members Member:

Example of School Staff Members Assignment Roster

Assignment Position/Name Operations Site(s)

Principal:

Assistant Principal (s):

Main Office:

Crisis Team Coordinator:

Back-up Coordinator:

Guidance Office:

Guidance Secretary:

Media Center:

Family Contact Guidance staff members:

School Social Worker:

Career Guidance Conference Room:

School Nurse:

Support Counseling for Students/ Staff members

Guidance staff members:

School Psychologist:

Example of Crisis Planning for Off-Campus Activities

Off-campus activities, including field trips, should follow a crisis protocol with the following information and essentials:

1. **Use name tags / personal identification** – note that these need to be worn on blouses or shirts rather than outer garments such as sweaters and coats which may be removed during bus trips. Write-bracelets might be considered for identification, particularly for younger children.

2. **A route map and itinerary should be left at the school** – school leadership and the school district transportation leadership should know the location of field trips or events and the proposed route to the location. Bus drivers should be instructed to follow the proposed route and to notify their transportation supervisor and the school if the route has to change.

3. **A manifest of riders in each bus or other vehicle should be left at the school before departure** - Students, staff members and volunteers should travel to and return from the activity site in the same vehicle. This should be an absolute requirement, because it is the only way to ensure that all students, staff members and volunteers are accounted for. Riders should be verified against the manifest when departing from the school or site and verified when loading for the trip back to the school.

4. **Determine who has cell phones.** It is desirable for someone in each vehicle to have a cell phone in addition to the bus radio transmitter. The cell phone numbers should be included on the manifest left at the school.

5. **Bus Emergency Kit**

    - Cell phone or other emergency communications equipment.

    - Rider roster (students, staff members, volunteers)

- Signs to display bus numbers

- Route maps with backup or emergency alternative routes noted

- Route maps to hospitals and crisis reunification sites

- Area maps

- Pen, paper or notebooks

- Stick-on name tags (or write-bracelets for younger students)

- First aid kit

- Emergency telephone numbers list

- District office (including cell phone numbers)

- Emergency medical services phone numbers if 911 service is not available in the area

- Law enforcement (State Police)

- Incident Report Forms

A Crisis When School is Not in Session

If a school administrator or other crisis response team member is notified of a crisis when school is not in session, the following steps should be taken:

1. Institute the communication contact protocol to disseminate information to appropriate staff members and parents.

2. Notify appropriate staff members by letter, email, text or telephone with information about the incident.

3. Be alert for any collateral after-effects of the incident, such as something carrying over into the school like retribution, for example.

4. If the crisis involved possible damage to the school or otherwise may have created unsafe conditions at the school, close school until the school has been determined to be safe.

5. Use news media of other means of communicating with parents regarding whether school will be open or closed.

Example of Incident Report Form

(Example of report to document crisis details – should be submitted to the superintendent or designee and reviewed by School District Crisis Response Team for debriefing and adjustments in the Crisis Management Plan or training)

Crises Response Team Report

Date of Report_____

School

_____

Staff Member or Members Filing the Incident Report

_____

_____

Description of incident (include date, time, place)

_____

_____

_____

_____

_____

_____

_____

_____

_____

_____

_____

Intervention/Response Activities

_____

_____

_____

_____

_____

_____

_____

_____

_____

Follow-up procedures (with student, with student body [if

appropriate], with staff)

_____

_____

_____

_____

_____

_____

_____

_____

Follow-up with parent(s)/guardian(s) of student(s) involved or community members

_____

_____

_____

_____

_____

_____

_____

_____

List agencies and others that provided support and assistance during the crisis

_____

_____

_____

_____

_____

_____

_____

Assessment of school's Crisis Plan and response

_____

_____

_____

_____

_____

_____

_____

_____

_____

_____

Other Information

_____

_____

_____

_____

_____

Attach an inventory of equipment or materials used during the crisis.

Reviewed by Principal:

_____

Date: _____

Post Crisis Incident Management and Recovery

Follow-up to Crisis Situations

The following information may be useful in the days and weeks following a crisis. Longer term follow-up procedures are also listed.

Short-term

1. Gather staff members and update them on any additional information/ procedures. Allow members opportunity to discuss feelings and reactions, with support staff members available.

2. In case of death, provide funeral/visitation information if affected family has given permission.

3. Identify students and staff members in need of follow-up support and, in accordance with the school's crisis management plan, assign staff members to monitor vulnerable students and other staff members.

4. Coordinate any ongoing counseling support for students on campus.

5. Announce ongoing support for students with place, time, and staff member facilitators.

6. Develop academic recovery plans, based on the nature of the crisis and duration of the crisis (NOTE: If the situation required a long-term school closure, questions may need to be directed to the state's department of education.)

Long-term Follow-up and Evaluation

1. Provide list of suggested readings to teachers, parents, and students to aid in the recovery.

2. Write thank-you notes to out-of-school district and community resource people who provided (or are still providing) support during the crisis.

3. Some students or staff members may experience "anniversary" reactions the following month or year on the date of the crisis, or when similar crises occur that remind them of the original crisis; therefore, be alert on crisis anniversaries and holidays.

Crisis Response Team Post-Crisis Debriefing

Post-incident debriefing is a process that reviews the school's and/or school district's response to the crisis and how it may be improved.

Example of Crisis Response Team Post-Crisis Debriefing

The systematic process of debriefing should include a review of each of the following. Ask for explanations to the answers and provide opportunities for staff members to express any frustrations and fears as well as suggestions.

1. **Initial understanding of crisis**

    Was the information accurate? Was the information complete? Were there misunderstandings? Was there confusion? Ask for explanations to the answers and provide opportunities for staff members to express any frustrations, fears as well as suggestions.

2. **Initial strategies and tactics**

    Were the first steps after the crisis appropriate? What else could have been done? What worked well? What could be done differently?

3. **Results of strategies and tactics**

    Were the intended results achieved? Were there any unintended consequences?

4. **Obstacles encountered**

    What? Who? Why? When? How? Were obstacles dealt with appropriately? Can anything be done to prevent obstacles in the future?

5. **Staff members**

    Was appropriate staff members notified in a timely manner? Was staff members properly prepared to respond in an appropriate manner? Did staff members respond in an appropriate manner? Does staff members need additional training?

6.   **Recommendations for improvement**

What lessons were learned? Are there policies and/or procedures that need to be amended? Does communication procedures and equipment need to be reviewed or updated?

7.   *Academic Recovery Review*

If the crisis required school closure for several days or weeks, how well did the academic recovery plan work? What was learned from implementing the academic recovery plan? What, if any, resources could have been better utilized? What resources should be gathered in preparation for a future crisis? Did students benefit from the academic recovery plan/strategies?

Maintaining Crisis Preparedness Following a Crisis

It is critically important for schools and school districts to maintain a high level of crisis preparedness throughout the year and revisit preparedness after a crisis. Contrary to popular opinion, there is a tendency for schools that have experienced a crisis to let its preparedness condition lapse out of an unfounded belief that a crisis will not happen again and from the misplaced feeling that the students and staff members will be traumatized if there are discussions about crisis management after a crisis.

Maintaining Crisis Awareness and Preparedness

One of the most effective means of maintaining awareness and preparedness is to periodically review the Crisis Management Plan. The following is an example checklist for a review of and access to a Crisis Management Plan.

1. Print updated crisis referral information in student handbook.

2. Print updated crisis referral information in faculty handbook.

3. Confirm membership of Crisis Response Team, filling vacancies that have occurred.

4. Review assigned roles and responsibilities of team members and revise, as needed.

5. Review overall Crisis Management Plan and update in light of changes in conditions and/or resources at the school or in the community.

6. Review Critical Incident Management procedures and update in light of changes in conditions and/or resources at the school or in the community.

7. Update faculty of any changes in Crisis Response Team membership and procedures including identification/intervention referral, for crisis response, critical incident response, and post-event.

8. Include review of Crisis Management Plan and related procedures in new staff members orientation.

9. Hold an all-staff members member in-service on the Crisis Management Plan and provide training in related topics on a regular basis.

10. Provide training locally or from the local emergency management agency and/or the state emergency management agency on prevention and crisis management.

Crisis Management Training

Schools and school districts can greatly benefit from established crisis management concepts and training modules.

The National Incident Management System (NIMS) is the national standard for crisis training and response. School staff members can be trained in the NIMS standards and learn to apply the Incident Command System (ICS) protocol as the organizing structure for their Critical Incident Response Plan. NIMS established procedures for priority-setting, interagency cooperation and the efficient flow of resources and information. NIMS established common standards of organization, procedures, communications and terminology among agencies. This unified command structure functions under the direction of the ICS and all agencies and organizations work together under this system to more effectively respond to any major critical incident. By adopting and utilizing this system, schools will respond to any critical incident with better communication and coordination with other responding agencies and organizations.

Incident Command System (ICS)

The Incident Command System provides a unified command in a multi-responder emergency in which all agencies which have a jurisdictional responsibility for multi-jurisdictional incident contribute to the process of:

1. Determining the overall objectives to gain control of the incident

2. Selecting strategies to achieve their objectives

3. Planning jointly for tactical activities

4. Integrating appropriate tactical operations

5. Making maximum use of all assigned resources

If school district or local school staff members need training in incident management and planning, the Federal Emergency Management Agency's Federal Management Institute offers National Incident Management System (NIMS) *on-line training*. Several modules are available on-line, but the following provide the basic understanding of incident command and communications.

IS-100.SC/IS-100: Introduction to Incident Command System

As an introduction to the Incident Command System (ICS), this course provides the foundation for higher level ICS training. This course describes the history, features and principles, and organizational structure of the Incident Command System. It also explains the relationship between ICS and the National Incident Management System (NIMS).

IS-242: Effective Communication

The ability to communicate effectively is a vital part of every emergency manager, planner, and responder's job. This course is designed to improve your communication skills. It addresses:

- Basic communication skills;

- How to communicate in an emergency;

- How to identify community-specific communication issues;

- How to use technology as a communication tool;

- Effective oral communication; and,

- How to prepare an oral presentation

E361: Multi-hazard Emergency Planning for Schools

This course describes emergency management operations, roles and duties; explains how to assess potential hazards that schools may face; and explains how to develop and test an Emergency Operations Plan that addresses all potential hazards. The course is designed for school administrators, principals, and first responders.

IS-360: Preparing for Mass Casualty Incidents: A Guide for Schools, Higher Education and Houses of Worship

This course provides leading practices and resources to assist elementary and secondary schools, institutions of higher education, and houses of worship in developing emergency plans for preparing for, responding to, and recovering from mass casualty incidents.

IS-362a: Multi-Hazard Emergency Planning for Schools

This course covers basic information about developing, implementing, and maintaining a school emergency operations plan (EOP). The goal of this course is to provide students with an understanding of the importance of schools having an EOP and basic information on how an EOP is developed, exercised, and maintained. The topics addressed in this course include:

- Understanding incident management.

- Forming the planning team.

- Understanding the situation.

- Developing a school emergency operations plan.

- Incorporating the Incident Command System principles and roles in the school emergency operations plan.

- Training, exercising, and maintaining the school emergency operations plan.

Earthquake Safety for Schools

This course provides an explanation of how earthquakes vary in scope and intensity and how each type of earthquake can cause a treat to schools. It includes elements that should be included in planning for and responding to an earthquake and it includes some myths about earthquakes that can be hazardous to schools.

IS-700: National Incident Management System (NIMS), an

Introduction

Homeland Security developed the National Incident Management System (NIMS). The NIMS provides a consistent nationwide template to enable all government, private-sector, and nongovernmental organizations to interact during domestic incidents. This course explains the purpose, principles, key components, and benefits of NIMS.

Chapter Five

Crisis Response Box

"If you fail to prepare, you prepare to fail."

-Attributed to several sources

The concept of a Crisis Response Box is for the purpose of a quick response to a crisis by housing all essential information and guidelines in one place and in a container that is mobile or stored digitally so it can be retrieved remotely. Some school districts are now loading all of the following information onto secured laptop or notebook computers or in secured "cloud" technology that can be retrieved through smartphones, laptops, or digital notebooks. The Crisis Response Box should contain the following items.

Aerial Photographs of Campus

An aerial perspective of the campus and the surrounding area is very helpful to all agencies involved in a critical incident, including police, fire and paramedic personnel. Local municipalities may be able to provide an aerial photo of schools and surrounding campus, and aerial photographs of school campuses may be download from a source such as Google Earth (check the date of the aerial photograph).

Campus Layout

It is important to maintain current, accurate blueprints, classroom layouts and floor plans of the school and grounds, including information about main leads for water, gas, electricity, cable, telephone, alarm and sprinkler systems, hazardous materials (e.g. science labs, storage areas, boiler room) location, elevators and entrances. This information is extremely helpful, especially during a "shelter-in-place" situation when students are locked in a classroom and/or other locations in the school. Information should be available on the layout of the school, including room numbers and whether or not there is a phone, intercom, cable television, e-mail, computers or cell phones in the classroom. On the campus layout diagram, it is also helpful to highlight areas that could pose a possible threat, such as the chemistry laboratory, biology laboratory or any welding and wood shop areas that could also become a location for explosions or that contain items that could be used as weapons. These items can be designated by color or symbol on the campus layout.

Blueprint of School Schools

Architectural blueprints of the school are important to a first responders such as a SWAT team and fire department, because they provide additional -- and more detailed – information than the simple classroom layout diagram. It is also helpful to show the location of the fire alarm turn-off, sprinkler system turn-off, utility shut-off valves, cable television shut-off and first aid supply boxes. This information may be critical, especially in the event of a bomb threat, intruder or unidentified odor or smoke. The plant manager for the school site and the principal and assistant principal should have quick access to the blueprints in a digital format and/or hard copy format. Grounds and maintenance staff members and assistant principals of the school should be familiar with these blueprints and their location.

Staff members Member Roster

A staff member roster should go into the Crisis Response Box. Teachers' names on the classroom layout diagram can help first responders. If this is not possible, each teacher's name should be matched with his or her classroom and a note should be included that denotes whether or not each teacher has a cell or land phone. This roster should identify any staff member with special medical needs (e.g., diabetes) who will require medications during a prolonged period and those with a disability who may require assistance in an evacuation. Someone in the front office should be assigned to pick up the visitor/volunteer/substitute teacher list in the event of a critical incident.

Keys or Card Access

The Crisis Response Box should also contain a master key and an extra set of keys. The keys must be clearly tagged. The keys should be placed in a locked container within the box to assure added security in case the box should end up in the wrong hands. Some schools have found it advantageous to keep the master key in a Key

Box (rapid entry system) outside of the school. This is a secured metal box that can easily be accessed by a code or a key without having to enter the school. This can prove especially helpful when it is not safe to enter the school or if a first responder needs access to the school. Further information on a Key Box can be obtained from the local fire department. School districts and schools with a card access system should have a very specific card distribution system protocol that includes procedures for card distribution, for appropriate use of the cards, for card retrieval when an employee leaves the school or school district, and for deactivation of the card system. The distribution system description should be in the Crisis Response Box.

As school districts move to keyless and card-less access to schools as well as digital access mechanisms, they should develop access procedures for crisis situations, as well as develop safeguards that signal when the digital system or systems have been compromised or fail.

Fire Alarm Turn-off Procedures

One of the lessons learned from Columbine was to make it easier to turn off the alarm. The loud alarm made it very difficult for first responders to hear instructions and directions. It took considerable time before someone who knew how to turn it off was able to do so. School officials learned that they cannot assume that the person who knows how to turn off the alarm will be logistically able to do so. If that person is inside the school, he or she might not be able to get to the shutoff mechanism; if that person is outside, it is possible that he or she might not be able to safely re-enter the school. As a result, a number of people need to know how to shut off the alarm, or it should be a system that can shut off remotely.

Sprinkler System Turn-off Procedures

Sprinkler systems may activate during a crisis. During the incident at Columbine, no one was readily available who knew how to immediately turn off the sprinkler system. As a result, hallways quickly filled with water, making it difficult for students to evacuate the school. In some places, the water reached dangerous levels in proximity to the electrical outlets -- water reaching such outlets could have caused many more injuries and possibly additional deaths. The

Crisis Response Box should include information on where shutoff valves are located in the school and the shutoff procedures.

Utility Shutoff Valves

Shutoff and access points of all utilities -- gas, electric and water – need to be clearly identified and their locations listed on the campus layout and floor plans so they can be quickly shut off in a crisis. If there is not a fire, the water should be shut off immediately to prevent flooding from the sprinkler system. Unless open electric or gas lines pose an immediate threat to life, the decision on whether to shut off these lines should be made by the Incident Command Officer or first responders. The Crisis Response Box needs to include this information on where shutoff valves are located in the school and the shut off procedures.

Cable Television, Satellite, Digital Feed Shut-off

If a school has a feed for an internal surveillance system or classroom monitors, using cable, satellite or a digital format, school staff members should be prepared to disable the system in a crisis, particularly during an intruder situation when the intruder has taken over much of the school. Several law enforcement officers involved in nationally televised shootings recommend that the feed be shut off so that any intruders on the inside will not be able to view the whereabouts of the SWAT team by tuning into a live feed on the school's monitors. If there is an intruder in the school, the decision to utilize or disable the system should be made by the first responders. On the other hand, in some other situations, the system can be helpful to provide those who are sheltered-in-place with up-to-date information or if the system can be accessed by first responders to view the location of intruders or to find the location of students and staff members. The Crisis Response Box needs to include this information.

Student and Staff members Member Photographs

Student and staff member photos can help in the essential task of identifying students injured, missing or deceased. Staff members should have access in the Crisis Response Box to copies of student and staff members member photo IDs, the most recent school yearbook (along with the additional photos of the newest incoming class) or a digitally stored file of student and staff members member photographs. If photos are digital, it could assist first responders if the photos were available on a CD, which should be included in the Crisis Response Box. Many law enforcement agencies and other first responders bring laptops to the scene and can thereby gain instant access to such photos, print them out, make copies and distribute them to other first responders. This could be critically important to locate and account for every student and staff member. *Be very mindful of FERPA restrictions on sharing student information.*

Incident Command System (ICS) Key Responders' Contact

Information

Names and phone numbers for all team participants involved in coordinating with the local emergency response system should be in the Crisis Response Box. Also, the names, phone numbers, email addresses, and text message contacts of other key staff members should be included.

Emergency Resource List

A list of individuals and organizations that can assist in a crisis should be prepared and included in the Crisis Response Box so that designated staff members can immediately begin to make phone calls to those on the list. Please note that any staff members member or volunteer enlisted to make the response phones to agencies and other community services must be pre-screened and receive training. This is an example of a list of contact phone numbers that should be in the Crisis Response Box.

1. Local emergency management

2. State emergency management

3. Local law enforcement

4. Local fire and rescue

5. Community counselors (A cadre of trained crisis intervention counselors should be identified to provide mental health a first aid during and following the crisis, including counselors from mental health services)

6. Local public health department

7. Local television and radio channels

8. National Organization for Victim Assistance (NOVA)

9. Parent representative(s) (The parent representatives should be trained to help fellow parents receive information, answer questions and maintain calm at the Parent Staging Area.)

Map of Streets

Crisis response planners need to review the traffic patterns and intersections that could be affected in a major crisis. Through this process, sites and locations can be identified where parents or guardians can retrieve their children after an incident. Also, this will assist in the identification and anticipation of traffic safety issues that school transportation staff members and other staff members and law enforcement will have to consider when directing students and staff members to safe areas. The map should be available digitally and/or hard copies for emergency responders and staff members. An emergency traffic plan should be developed that is capable of protecting emergency response routes and accommodating traffic and parking needs for parents, students, emergency responders and the news media. The map should illustrate these planned routes as well as:

1. The streets surrounding the school

2. Intersections near the school

3. Vacant lots near the school

4. Possible relocation sites and schools for students and staff

    members

5. Location of major utilities near the routes

6. Possible hazards in or near the routes

Evacuation Routes and Reunification Sites

Maps with evacuation and alternate evacuation routes along with reunification and secondary reunification sites should be stored in the Crisis Response Box. The maps will indicate which routes students and staff members will likely follow and the destination they are seeking. This is important in order to identify them, or, if they are missing, to determine where along the route they might be found. Be aware, however, that during some crisis the evacuation routes may have to be altered. That is why it is critically important to have alternate routes and reunification sites. All classrooms at Columbine, for example, had evacuation plans, but with two students shooting throughout the entire school, evacuating the school was itself a dangerous venture. In the Jonesboro, Arkansas incident, two boys opened fire while students evacuated the school during a false fire alarm. Other factors may alter evacuation routes. In a chemical spill, for instance, how the winds are blowing will determine where to evacuate. Thus, it is important to have at least two predetermined evacuation routes identified and included in the Crisis Response Box.

Designated Command Post and Staging Areas

First responders involved in several of the recent school crisis situations recommend that schools and first responders plan for three distinct staging areas, in addition to the Command Post for the Incident Command Officer: first responders' staging area; news media staging area; and parent staging area. The staging areas prevent chaos and allow the school to keep track of students and staff members, as well as providing access to injured students. Maps of all command posts and staging areas listing each corresponding phone number and other contact information should be included in the Crisis Response Box.

Student Disposition Forms and Crisis Data Cards

Because of the possibility of hundreds of parents descending upon a school to reunite with their children while the school is trying to account for each student's whereabouts, schools should have forms to keep track of which students have been released and to whom: parents, relatives, emergency personnel or the hospital. It is suggested that a set of release forms (enough to cover the entire school census) be stored in the Crisis Response Box, or a laptop or other digital means of collecting and storing this information. Additionally, if possible, it is helpful to have a set of student crisis data cards included in the Crisis Response Box or the same information in a digital format. Having all the data stored on a CD, flash-drive or laptop/notebook is an accessible way of containing and accessing the information. Crisis information can also be stored, updated and retrieved electronically either from the school or a remote site.

Student Attendance Roster

One of the most difficult challenges in a crisis is accounting for all students. Teachers should have a readily accessible listing of all pupils in their charge, either in a written format or in an accessible digital format. Teachers should also be instructed to take their classroom attendance list (printed or digital) with them during an evacuation. A system should be developed to retrieve these lists from teachers when it is safe and feasible. Someone should be assigned to place that day's attendance roster into the Crisis Response Box or digitally *each morning*. This critical information can then be available for school staff members and first responders during an emergency. It is not enough to simply have the classroom rosters; first responders need to know which students were actually in school at the time of the crisis. Some schools store all student attendance and information data digitally, thus making remote access to the data possible.

Inventory of Staff members Resources

The staff member inventory of special skills, experiences and training should be included in the Crisis Response Box. Experience, skills, and training in the following areas could offer needed assistance: medical and triage experience, bilingual capabilities, grief counseling background, search and rescue training, hostage negotiations, first aid/CPR certification and volunteer firefighter or reserve police officer/deputy.

List of Students and Staff members with Special Needs

A list should also be included in the Crisis Response Box that identifies those students and staff members who need special assistance (e.g., blind and deaf students and those who need wheelchairs, crutches and braces) and/or with special medical needs (e.g., diabetes) that will require medications during a prolonged period.

First Aid Supplies Location

Sets of first aid supplies should be located throughout the campus. Storage location maps should be included in the Crisis Response box.

Crisis First Aid Supplies

The FBI Academy recommends that schools be aware of information from the *Lessons Learned Summit* regarding first aid supplies. In the Jonesboro, Arkansas shooting, large bins of first aid supplies were readily accessible on the school grounds and are credited with saving two children's lives and preventing others from going into shock. First aid supplies were situated inside and outside of the school school in anticipation of an earthquake because the school property is located on a fault line. The accessibility of these supplies proved to be lifesaving. Some schools have stationed first aid boxes in every classroom with basic emergency aid instructions to treat various injuries. Some schools have created Medical Go Kits that include standard First Aid supplies and located throughout the school and assigned to specified staff members. This information should be included in the Crisis Response Box.

Quick Reference Information Checklist for Crisis Response Box

Maps

✓ Streets surrounding school

✓ Intersections near school

✓ Vacant lots

✓ Possible evacuation hazards or impediments

✓ Location of nearby schools that can be used for temporary housing (e.g., community gym, church, auditorium, etc.)

Campus Layout and Blueprint of School

✓ Room numbers, phone numbers, computers, e-mail, cable TV

✓ Threat areas (e.g., chemistry and biology labs, shops, gasoline storage areas, boiler rooms)

Teacher/Staff members Member Roster

✓ Room and cell phone numbers

✓ Staff members directory

✓ Copy of employee photo Identifies

Fire Alarm Turn-off Procedures

✓ How and where located

Sprinkler System Turn-off Procedures

✓ How and where located

Utility Shut-off Valves

- ✓ Electric
- ✓ Gas
- ✓ Water
- ✓ Where and how to shut off

Gas Line and Utility Lines Lay-Out

- ✓ This information can be provided by school district service centeror local utility departments

First Aid Supplies

- ✓ Location and how to access

Designated Command Posts

- ✓ Identify Area for Law Enforcement, Emergency Personnel
- ✓ Receiving Area for Parents
- ✓ Receiving Area for Press

Cable Television or Surveillance Camera Shut-off or Monitoring

- ✓ Identify where and how

Student and Staff members Member Photographs

- ✓ Copy of photo IDs of students
- ✓ Current yearbook

Evacuation Sites

- ✓ Maps with routes to at least two evacuation sites; should also be posted in classrooms.

Disposition Forms

- ✓ Set of forms for parents/guardians/hospitals/ER personnel to sign when a student has been released to them.

Student Attendance Roster

- ✓ Roster should be entered in the box daily
- ✓ Teachers bring their classroom attendance sheet to evacuation site

List of Students with Special Needs

- ✓ List of students with special medical needs requiring medications
- ✓ List of students with a disability requiring assistance in an evacuation
- ✓ Student emergency card data

Chapter Six

Crisis Threat Assessment

When written in Chinese, the word 'crisis' is composed of two characters. One represents danger and the other represents opportunity.
-John F. Kennedy

What is a Threat?

A threat is an expression of intent to do harm or act out violently against another person. A threat can be spoken, written, or physical – for example, motioning with one's hands as though shooting at another person.

All threats are not equal. However, all threats must be taken seriously and evaluated. Most threats are made anonymously or under a false name. Because threat assessment relies heavily on evaluating the person's demeanor, motive, background, personality, lifestyle, and resources, identifying the person is necessary for an informed assessment to be made -- and also so criminal charges can be brought if the threat is serious enough to warrant prosecution. If the person's identity cannot be determined, the response will have to be based on an assessment of the threat and any previous threats from the same person or under similar circumstances. A threat that was considered low risk may be rated as more serious if new information suggests the person is dangerous, or conversely, an assessment of high risk may be scaled down if the person is identified and found not to have the intent, ability, means, or motive to carry out the threat.

Motivation for Threats

According to the FBI, threats are made for a variety of reasons. A threat may be a warning signal, a reaction to fear of punishment or some other anxiety, or a demand for attention. It may be intended to taunt; to intimidate; to assert power or control; to punish; to manipulate or coerce; to frighten; to terrorize; to compel someone to do something; to strike back for an injury, injustice or slight; to disrupt someone's or some institution's life; to test authority, or to protect oneself. The emotions that underlie a threat can be love; hate; fear; rage; or desire for attention, revenge, excitement, or recognition. Motivation can never be known with complete certainty, but to the extent possible, understanding motive is a key element in evaluating a threat. A threat may reflect the person's mental and emotional state at the time the threat was made, but it is important to remember that a state of mind can be temporarily but strongly influenced by circumstances, such as alcohol or drugs, domestic dispute, etc.

Signposts and Signals of Threats

In general, people do not switch instantly from nonviolence to violence. Reports by the FBI and the Secret Service indicate that nonviolent people do not "snap" or decide on the spur of the moment to meet a problem by using violence. Instead, the path toward violence is an evolutionary one, with signs along the way. A threat is observable behavior; others may be brooding about frustration or disappointment, fantasies of destruction or revenge, in conversations, writings, drawings, and other actions.

Types of Threats

Threats can be classed in four categories, according to the FBI and Secret Service: direct, indirect, veiled, or conditional.

1. A *direct threat* identifies a specific act against a specific target and is delivered in a straightforward, clear, and explicit manner: "I am going to place a bomb in the school's gym."

2. An *indirect threat* tends to be vague, unclear, and ambiguous. The plan, the intended victim, the motivation, and other aspects of the threat are masked or equivocal: "If I wanted to, I could kill everyone at this school!" While violence is implied, the threat is phrased tentatively -- "If I wanted to" – and suggests that a violent act COULD occur, not that it WILL occur.

3. A *veiled threat* is one that strongly implies but does not explicitly threaten violence. "We would be better off without you around anymore" clearly hints at a possible violent act, but leaves it to the potential victim to interpret the message and give a definite meaning to the threat.

4. A *conditional threat* is the type of threat often seen in extortion cases. It warns that a violent act will happen unless certain demands or terms are met: "If you don't pay me one million dollars, I will place a bomb in the school."

Factors in Threat Assessment

Specific, plausible and accurate details are a critical factor in evaluating a threat, according to the FBI. The following includes details and guidelines from the FBI Threat Assessment protocol. It is provided here only for information purposes and not as guiding principles for decision-making in threat circumstances, because each threat situation is different.

Threat Assessment

Threat assessment details can include the identity of the intended victim or victims; the reason for making the threat; the means – weapon or device; method by which it is to be carried out; the date, time, and place where the threatened act will occur; and concrete information about plans or preparations that have already been made. Specific details can indicate that thought, planning, and preparatory steps have already been taken. This places the threat at a higher risk that the person will follow through on his or her threat. It is also important to determine if there is a history of this type of threat, either by this person or someone the person knows and has known in the past.

A lack of detail suggests the person may not have thought through all of the contingencies, has not actually taken steps to carry out the threat, and may not seriously intend violence but is overtly expressing anger or frustration or is seeking to frighten or intimidate a particular victim, a school, or disrupt a school's events or routine. Details that are specific but not logical or plausible may indicate a less serious threat. For example, a student phones in a threat that he intends to pack and explode a 1,000 pounds of TNT under the bleachers in the gym at noon. The threat is detailed and states a specific time, place, and weapon, but the threat action is not plausible. A threat this unrealistic is obviously unlikely to be carried out. However, a threat that includes some of the basic elements such as time, location but vagueness about the weapon or device must be taken seriously.

The emotional content of a threat can be an important clue to the person's mental state, according to the forensic studies enumerated by the FBI. Emotions are conveyed by melodramatic words -- "I hate you!" "You have ruined my life!" "May God have mercy on your soul!" "I hate that school." Though emotionally charged threats can tell the threat assessor something about the temperament of the person, they are not typically a measure of danger unless accompanied by specific information about a threat of action.

Precipitating stressors are incidents, circumstances, reactions, or situations which can trigger a threat. The precipitating event may seem insignificant and have no direct relevance to the threat, but nonetheless becomes a catalyst. For example, a male student has been rebuffed by a female student, which seems innocuous, but it sets off an emotional chain reaction leading the student to threaten another student at school that day -- possibly something he has thought about in the past. The impact of a precipitating event will obviously depend on pre-disposing factors such as underlying personality traits, mental health status, life experiences, and temperament. Accordingly, information about a temporary "trigger" must be considered together with broader information about these underlying factors, such as a student's vulnerability to loss and depression.

Levels of Threat Risk

✓ **Low Level of Threat**: A threat which poses a minimal risk.

Threat is vague and indirect.

1. Information contained within the threat is inconsistent, implausible or lacks detail.

2. Threat lacks realism.

3. Content of the threat suggests person is unlikely to

carry it out.

✓ **Medium Level of Threat**: A threat which could be carried out, although it may not appear entirely realistic.

1. Threat is more direct and more concrete than a low level threat.

2. Wording in the threat suggests that the person has given some thought to how the act will be carried out.

3. There may be a general indication of a possible place and time (though these signs still fall well short of a detailed plan).

4. There is no strong indication that the person has taken preparatory steps, although there may be some veiled reference or ambiguous or inconclusive evidence pointing to that possibility -- an allusion to a book or movie that shows the planning of a violent act.

5. There may be a specific statement seeking to convey that the threat is not empty: "I'm serious!" or "I really mean this!"

✓ **High Level of Threat**: A threat that appears to pose an imminent and serious danger to the safety of others.

1. Threat is direct, specific and plausible.

2. Threat suggests concrete steps have been taken toward carrying it out, for example, statements indicating that the person has acquired or practiced with a weapon or has had the victim or school under surveillance.

Example: *"At eight o'clock tomorrow morning, I intend to shoot the principal. That's when he is in the office by himself. I have a 9mm. Believe me, I know what I am doing. I am sick and tired of the way he runs this school."*

This threat is direct, specific as to the victim, motivation, weapon, place, and time, and indicates that the person knows his target's schedule and has made preparations to act on the threat.

Students Who May Represent a Potential Threat Risk

In the event that a staff members member has reason to believe that a student may represent a potential threat to others, the following is a list of possible actions. These steps apply only to situations in which the student is presenting *no immediate threat*.

1. Take all comments about doing harm to others seriously, especially if details about how the acts are to be carried out are shared.

2. Immediately report concerns to an administrator.

3. Under no circumstances should an untrained person attempt to assess the severity of the risk; all assessment of threats, attempts, or other risk factors must be left to the appropriate professionals.

NOTE: It is important to avoid inappropriately labeling or stigmatizing individual students because they appear to fit a specific profile or set of early warning indicators. It is appropriate to be worried about a student, but it's not appropriate to overreact and jump to conclusions and accuse a student of a serious act or intentions without knowing or having relevant information.

Chapter Seven

Early Warning Signs

Prevention is better than a cure.

-Desiderius Erasmus

Predictability of Violent Behavior

It is not always possible to predict behavior that will lead to violence. However, educators, parents, and even students can recognize certain early warning signs. In some situations and for some youth, different combinations of events, behaviors, and emotions may lead to aggressive or violent behavior toward self or others. A good rule of thumb is to assume that these warning signs, especially when they are presented in combination, indicate a need for further analysis to determine an appropriate intervention.

Research indicates that most students who become violent toward self or others feel rejected and psychologically victimized. In most cases, students exhibit aggressive behavior early in life and, if not provided support, will continue a progressive developmental pattern toward severe aggression or violence. However, research also shows that when students have a positive, meaningful connection to an adult – whether at home, in school, or in the community -- the potential for violence is reduced significantly. This also applies to a positive school climate. Students with adjustment problems or mental health problems are more likely to respond well to the school setting if the school's climate includes elements such as connectedness, support, positive communication, and participation (McGiboney, 2016).

Excerpts from the booklet *Early Warning, Timely Response* (a publication from the United States Department of Education) provide valuable insight into early assessment of signs that a student is struggling with many personal issues. None of these signs enumerated below alone is sufficient for predicting aggression and violence. Moreover, it is inappropriate – and potentially harmful – to use the early warning signs as a checklist against which to evaluate individual students without considering all of the elements that may contribute to the student's ideation and behavior. Rather, the early warning signs are offered only as an aid in identifying and referring students who may need assistance. School must ensure that staff members only use the early warning signs for identification and referral purposes – only trained professionals should make diagnoses in consultation with the student's parents or guardian.

Warning Sign Indicators

The following early warning signs are presented with the following qualifications: They are not equally significant and they are not presented in order of seriousness. The early warning signs may include:

1. **Social withdrawal**

   In some situations, gradual and eventually complete withdrawal from social contacts can be an important indicator of a troubled student, particularly if there is a significant and long-term change from interaction to withdrawal. Social withdrawal may stem from feelings of depression, rejection, persecution, unworthiness, lack of confidence, or a change in self-image.

2. **Excessive feelings of isolation and being alone**

   The majority of students who appear to be friendless are not violent. In fact, these feelings are sometimes characteristic of students who may be troubled, withdrawn, or have internal issues that hinder development of social affiliations.

3. **Excessive feelings of rejection**

   In the process of growing up, and in the course of social development, most students will at some time experience emotionally painful rejection. Their responses to rejection will depend on many background factors. Without support, they may be at risk of expressing their emotional distress in negative ways including violence toward others or toward themselves. Some aggressive students who are rejected by non-aggressive peers seek out other students like them who, in turn, reinforce their violent ideas, thoughts and actions.

4. **Being a victim of violence**

    Students who are victims of violence, including physical
    or sexual abuse in the community, school, or home are
    sometimes at risk of becoming violent toward themselves
    or others.

5. **Feelings of being picked on and persecuted**

    The student who feels constantly picked on, teased,
    bullied, singled out for ridicule, and humiliated at home,
    in the community or at school may initially withdraw
    socially. If not given adequate support in addressing these
    feelings, some students may vent them in inappropriate
    ways, including possible aggression or violence.

6. **Low school interest and poor academic performance**

    Poor school achievement can be the result of many
    factors. It is important to consider whether there is a
    drastic change in performance and/or poor performance
    becomes a chronic condition that limits the student's
    capacity to learn. In some situations, such as when the low
    achiever feels frustrated, unworthy, chastised, or
    denigrated, acting out and aggressive behaviors may
    occur. It is important to assess the emotional and cognitive
    reasons for the academic performance change to determine
    the true nature of the problem.

7. **Expression of violence in writings and drawings**

    Students often express their thoughts, feelings, desires,
    and intentions in their drawings and in stories, poetry, and
    other written expressive forms. It is not uncommon,
    however, for some students, particularly young students or
    middle school age students, to produce work about violent
    themes that for the most part are harmless when taken in
    context. However, an over representation of violence in
    writings and drawings that is directed at specific
    individuals (family members, peers, other adults)
    consistently over time, may signal emotional problems
    and the potential for violence toward self or others.

Because there is a real danger in misdiagnosing such a sign, it is important to seek the guidance of a qualified professional, such as a school psychologist, counselor, or other mental health specialist, to determine its meaning.

8. **Uncontrolled anger**

Everyone gets angry; anger is a natural emotion. However, anger that is expressed frequently and intensely in response to minor irritants may signal potential violent behavior toward self or others.

9. **Patterns of impulsive and chronic hitting, intimidating, and bullying behaviors**

Students often engage in acts of shoving and mild aggression. However, some mildly aggressive behaviors such as constant hitting and bullying of others that occur early in student's lives, if left unattended, might later escalate into more serious behaviors. Students who attend schools that have a negative school climate are more prone to exposure to behavior like bullying and if adults do not care enough to prevent and intervene to stop the bullying they can then become the object of aggressive behavior by the victim of bullying.

10. **History of discipline problems**

Chronic behavior and disciplinary problems both in school and at home may suggest that underlying emotional needs are not being met. These unmet needs may be manifested in acting out and aggressive behaviors. These problems may set the stage for the student to violate norms and rules, defy authority, disengage from school, and engage in aggressive behaviors with other children and adults.

11. **Past history of violent and aggressive behavior**

Unless provided with support and counseling, a student who has a history of aggressive or violent behavior or who is exposed to a history of such behavior is likely to repeat or express those behaviors. Aggressive and violent acts may, for example, be directed toward other individuals, be expressed in cruelty to animals, or include fire setting. Students who show an early pattern of antisocial behavior frequently and across multiple settings are particularly at risk for future aggressive and antisocial behavior. Similarly, students who engage in overt behaviors such as bullying, generalized aggression and defiance, and covert behaviors such as stealing, cruelty, vandalism, lying, cheating, and fire setting also are at risk for more serious aggressive behavior. Students who engage in aggression and drug abuse at an early age (before age 12) are more likely to show violence later on than are students who begin such behavior at an older age. In the presence of such signs it is important to review the student's history with behavioral experts and seek parents' observations and insights.

12. **Intolerance for differences and prejudicial attitudes**

All students have likes and dislikes. However, an intense prejudice toward others based on race, ethnicity, religion, language, gender, sexual orientation, ability, and/or physical appearance – when coupled with other factors – may lead to violent assaults against those who are perceived to be different. Membership in hate groups or the willingness to victimize individuals with disabilities or health problems also should be treated as early warning signs.

13. **Drug use and alcohol use**

In addition to being unhealthy behaviors, drug use and alcohol use can reduce self-control and result in student behavior that is more aggressive than usual toward other students or toward self.

14. **Affiliation with gangs**

Gangs that support anti-social values and behaviors, including extortion, intimidation, and acts of violence toward other students, cause fear and stress among other students. Students who are influenced by these groups -- those who emulate and copy their behavior, as well as those who become affiliated with them -- may adopt these values and act in violent or aggressive ways in certain situations.

15. **Inappropriate access to, possession of, and use of firearms**

Students with emotional or social adjustment issues who have access to firearms can have an increased risk for aggressive behavior. Families can reduce inappropriate access and use by restricting, monitoring, and supervising student's access to firearms and other weapons. Students who have a history of aggression, impulsiveness, or other emotional problems should not have access to firearms and other weapons.

Identifying and Responding to Imminent Warning Signs

Unlike early warning signs, imminent warning signs indicate that a student is very close to behaving in a way that is potentially dangerous to self and/or to others. Imminent warning signs require an immediate response. No single warning sign can predict that a dangerous act will occur. Rather, imminent warning signs usually are presented as a sequence of overt, serious, hostile behaviors or threats directed at peers, staff members, or other individuals. Often, imminent warning signs are evident to more than one staff member.

Imminent warning signs may include:

1. Serious physical fighting with peers or family members

2. Severe destruction of property

3. Severe rage for seemingly minor reasons

4. Detailed threats of lethal violence

5. Possession and/or use of firearms and other weapons

6. Other self-injurious behaviors or threats of suicide

When warning signs indicate that danger is imminent, safety must always be the first and foremost consideration. Action must be taken immediately, such as notification of parents, school and community mental health staff members, and law enforcement, if necessary for the safety of the student or others.

Chapter Eight

Crisis Response Procedures

A wise person does at once, what a fool does at last. Both do the
same thing, just at different times.
-Sir John Dalberg-Acton

This chapter includes numerous examples of response procedures for various crisis situations that may arise in school settings and/or in communities near schools. The examples do not include all possible crisis situations, but they do represent the types of crises that most often occur and that pose the most danger for students and staff members. Each crisis situation listed includes examples of basic procedures most pertinent to the crisis. Each school should include possible local crisis situations that may be unique to the community and location of the school in the community. As mentioned earlier in this book, local emergency responders, law enforcement, mental health and public health officials should be included in the development of crisis response procedures.

Crisis Emergency Kits

All schools should build at least two crisis emergency kits that are easily transported. These should be readily available during a crisis evacuation or during other types of crises. One kit should be kept in the administrative offices and the others at an easily accessible but secure location in other sections of the school. An administrator and two designated staff members should take the kits whenever the school is evacuated or students and staff members are relocated. During an evacuation one kit should be taken to the family reunification site.

Reminder: the kits should be stored in safe and secure locations so as not to be readily accessible by an offender.

Example of an Emergency Kit Contents

1.   A copy of the Crisis Management Plan

2.   10 writing tablets and pens/pencils

3.   Laptops/notebooks/smartphones

4.   10 permanent makers

5.   500 plain white peel-off name tag stickers (used to identify injured students or staff members)

6.   Student release/sign-out sheets (keep a log of sign-outs digitally, if possible)

7.   List of students on off-campus trips

8.   Several sets of safety gloves

9.   Floor Plan of the school

10. Site Plan of the grounds and surrounding areas

11. Street maps of the area

12. Copies of photographs of the school (interior and exterior)

13. Copies of student and staff members emergency contact/release information

14. Information regarding any students and staff members with medical problems that may be impacted by the evacuation or emergency

15. Most recent yearbook

16. Flashlight and extra batteries

17. Bullhorn and extra batteries

18. Cell phone and/or walkie-talkie

19. Basic First-Aid kit

20. Lightweight blankets

21. At least two orange or yellow safety vests

Crisis Evacuation and Reunification Protocol

In some situations, it may be necessary to evacuate a school. The only safe evacuation is an orderly, well-planned evacuation with alternative routes.

Preparedness

1. Identify more than one outside assembly point at least 1,000 feet away from school in the event it becomes necessary to evacuate the school campus. Where the surrounding terrain, schools, streets, etc. make it impossible to assemble 1,000 feet away from the school, make sure all alternative assembly points are as far away from the school as possible (e.g., athletic fields, parks, businesses, etc.).

2. Establish the evacuation routes to the assembly points on an evacuation plan.

3. Provide for the special evacuation needs of the permanently or temporarily disabled.

4. Maintain a copy of the evacuation plan at the administrative offices and other areas of the school, as well as digitally, so that teachers and administrators can evacuate with it and be able to refer to it once outside.

5. Orient staff members, faculty and students to the evacuation routes, specific duties, requirements, and responsibilities during an evacuation.

6. Periodically test the public address system as the primary means of notifying school occupants. Establish alternate means of announcing an evacuation in the event of public address system failure such as cell phones or bullhorns.

7. Maps indicating primary and secondary evacuation routes should be posted in all classrooms.

8. Practice the evacuation

Response

1. Teachers should bring their classroom student attendance records with them to the evacuation site (s).

2. Teachers should ensure that their students are out of the classrooms and restrooms and workrooms.

3. The first student in line should be instructed to hold open the exit door(s) until all persons in the class have evacuated.

4. Classes should proceed to the designated holding areas/evacuation sites. Once there, teachers should make a note of students who are not present and furnish those names to school administrators immediately.

5. The principal and/or designee should notify school transportation to begin routing school buses to the evacuation site(s), if needed. Some situations will require alternative or delayed means of transporting students home, so a staging area for the school buses should be identified.

6. Designated staff members should notify local emergency agencies and the School Police and/or local police Department to proceed to the assembly site and set up a management center and traffic routing procedures.

7. The principal and/or designee should notify school transportation to begin routing school buses to the evacuation site(s), if needed. Some situations will require alternative or delayed means of transporting students home, so a staging area for the school buses should be identified.

8. Designated staff members should notify local emergency agencies and the School Police and/or local police Department to proceed to the assembly site and set up a management center and traffic routing procedures.

9. Teachers should remain with their class until administrators sound the "all clear" signal.

10. Use the "card" system, which includes giving all teachers three color-coded cards: Green Card-all students are present; Yellow Card-students are missing but the teacher knows where they can be found; Red Card-teacher needs immediate assistance.

11. Assign staff members at the assembly site to collect critical information and to manage and monitor students at the assembly site(s).

12. School administrators should collect lists of unaccounted for students from staff members and compare with the daily attendance absentee list and notify first responders of missing students.

13. Identify the location of classes in the evacuation site(s) to facilitate an orderly transfer of students to their parents.

14. Direct parents to the assembly site(s) to pick up students. The news media can be used to inform parents of the situation and that they may pick their students up at the assembly site or wait for them to be brought home via school bus. This will be determined based on circumstances.

15. Set up a sign-out area at the assembly site(s) and release students only to pre-determined authorized persons using the sign-out procedure.

16. Instruct parents or guardians to leave the site to make room for others once they have signed out their student.

17. As conditions allow, monitor the assembly site so students can begin loading unto buses, and a manifest should be established to account for all students riding buses.

18. Students not riding buses and not picked up by parents or guardians should remain in the evacuation site(s) until an authorized person arrives to pick them up.

19. Maintain contact with police/fire department(s) to stay informed about conditions at the school site.

20. Administrative staff members, with assistance from the School System Information Office and/or the Crisis Management Team, should prepare a written statement to be sent home with students.

NOTE: When students and staff members are away from the school on school-sponsored trips, staff members should follow procedures for monitoring students and should become acclimated to evacuation routes at the location, school, facility or venue that is being visited. Staff members should take note of marked exits and emergency exits and instruct students to stay together and reunite at a designated location in case they become separated.

Accident, Illness, and/or Injury Protocol

The names and location of staff members certified in First Aid and CPR should be made available to every school employee in the school. A fully stocked First Aid Kit should be readily available at all times.

In Critical Situations

1. Notify administrative staff members.

2. Activate the Crisis Management Team and begin the process of identifying injured students or staff members and triage the situation.

3. Notify local police or sheriff.

4. Call emergency medical services **(911).**

5. Administer first aid by a trained staff member.

6. Clear the area around the injured student.

7. Limit activity in the vicinity of the affected student(s) and relocate uninjured students as necessary.

8. Assign staff members to make certain the school parking lot area is clear so first responders can reach the school with equipment.

9. Assign staff members to stand outside of the school to receive first responders in order to direct them to the student(s).

10. Call family members.

11. Call the school district school district office.

12. Administrative staff members, with assistance from the school district office and/or the Crisis Management Team,

should prepare a written statement to be sent home with students.

In Critical Situations with Several Injured or Ill

1. Notify administrative staff members.

2. Call 911 where available or call emergency services. where available or call emergency services.

3. Administer first aid by trained staff members.

4. Activate the Crisis Management Team and begin the process of identifying injured students or staff members and triage the situation.

5. Clear the area around the injured student.

6. Limit activity in the vicinity of the affected student and relocate uninjured students as necessary.

7. Assign staff members to make certain the school parking lot area is clear so first responders can reach the school with equipment.

8. Assign staff members to stand outside of the school to receive first responders in order to direct them to the student(s).

9. Assign staff members to help control and contain the area.

10. Call family members.

11. Call the school district school district office.

12. Administrative staff members, with assistance from the school district office and/or the Crisis Management Team, should prepare a written statement to be sent home with students.

Explosive Device Threats/Suspicious Packages Protocol

Daily Precautions

1. Each morning, all school staff members should check their areas for any suspicious packages or items.

2. All rooms should be locked when not in use.

3. Cleaning and maintenance personnel should lock all doors after cleaning rooms, cafeteria, media center, etc.

4. Persons who handle mail and packages should be alert to unusual packages or letters (i.e., excess postage on a small package or letter indicates that the object was not weighed by the Post Office; no postage or non-canceled postage; handwritten notes such as "to be opened by Mr. Smith;" leaks, stains or sharp points, wires, etc.).

Response to Active Event

1. Suspicious items should never be moved or touched.

2. School administrators should be immediately notified if a suspicious item is found and the area should be isolated until law enforcement personnel have made an assessment of the item.

3. Crisis Management Team members should look for other suspicious items and report such items to school administrators or emergency personnel without touching or handling the items.

4. A threat analysis is conducted by emergency management agency or law enforcement.

5. If evacuation is warranted based on the analysis, staff members and students should move to predetermined assembly points at least 1,000 feet away from the school using predetermined routes and exits (**NOTE**: administrators must re-direct classes if the predetermined

routes pass near the alleged location of the explosive threat).

6. Ensure that all staff members and students have left the school. Check hallways, restrooms, lounges, cafeterias, auditoriums, and gymnasiums.

7. Designated staff members should take the Crisis Emergency Kit to the evacuation site(s).

8. Use bullhorns or adult runners to communicate and confirm that the school has been evacuated. Do not use portable radios, cellular phones, digital phones, or any other electronic devices. These devices have the capacity to detonate an explosive device.

9. Designated staff members should account for all students by checking with teachers in the evacuation site(s).

10. All staff members and students must remain in the evacuation site until the "all clear" signal is sent.

11. Call the school district school district office.

12. If the school has to be evacuated away from the school campus use the "card" system, which includes giving all teachers three color-coded cards: Green Card-all students are present; Yellow Card-students are missing but the teacher knows where they can be found; Red Card-teacher needs immediate assistance.

13. Assign staff members at the evacuation site to collect critical information and to manage and monitor students at the assembly site(s).

14. School administrators should collect lists of unaccounted for students from staff members and compare with the daily attendance absentee list and notify first responders of missing students.

15. Identify the location of classes in the evacuation site(s) to facilitate an orderly transfer of students to their parents.

16. Direct parents to the assembly site(s) to pick up students. The news media can be used to inform parents of the situation and that they may pick their students up at the assembly site or wait for them to be brought home via school bus. This will be determined based on circumstances.

17. Set up a sign-out area at the assembly site(s) and release students only to pre-determined authorized persons using the sign-out procedure.

18. Instruct parents or guardians to leave the site to make room for others once they have signed out their student.

19. As conditions allow, monitor the assembly site so students can begin loading unto buses, and a manifest should be established to account for all students riding buses.

20. Students not riding buses and not picked up by parents or guardians should remain in the evacuation site(s) until an authorized person arrives to pick them up.

21. Maintain contact with police/fire department(s) to stay informed about conditions at the school site.

22. Administrative staff members, with assistance from the school district information office and/or the Crisis Management Team, should prepare a written statement to be sent home with students.

Bomb or Explosive Device Threat Call Checklist
(IMPORTANT: Place a copy of the checklist next to school phones)

Ask the Caller:

1. Where is the bomb right now?

2. What does the bomb look like?

3. When is the bomb going to explode?

4. What kind of bomb is it?

5. What will cause the bomb to explode?

6. Did you place the bomb?

7. Why?

8. What is your name?

Exact Wording of Bomb Threat:

Caller Information: Sex: Race: Age: Length of Call:

Caller's Voice (check appropriate descriptions): Calm   Nasal
Slurred   Soft   Angry   Whispered   Stutter   Loud   Accent
Excited   lisp   Disguised   Laughter   Slow   Cracking
Raspy   Crying   Normal   Familiar Voice?   Who?

Background Sounds: Traffic   Voices   Music   House Noises
Static   Clear   Office Noises   Factory   Long Distance
Machinery   PA System   Other:

Threat Language: Well-Spoken   Incoherent   Offensive Words
Message Read   Taped   Irrational

Notifications: 911/School Police/Local Police/School district office
Other

Calls Received By:
Name:
Title/Position:
Telephone Number:
Date:

Additional Notes/Comments/Opinions about the Caller:

Weather Related Crisis Protocol

Develop a protocol to determine what should be monitored to determine if schools should be closed due to pending or possible weather conditions.

Preparations

1. Participate in National Weather Service (NWS) briefings.
   - ✓ Contact the NWS for instructions on how to participate in the briefings. If inclement weather is possible and throughout a weather event, the NWS conducts daily weather briefings that convey projections and conditions of the weather. At the end of the briefings, participates may ask questions about the forecast and conditions in the area. To sign up for the NWS briefings, the staff members member must represent the school district.)

2. Monitor NWS and other updated reports of pending or possible weather conditions.

   - ✓ **Each school and district office should have at least one Digital Weather/Hazard Alert Monitor** (the monitor also sounds alerts for other hazards, such as chemical spills).

3. Understand and recognize the difference between "Watch" and "Warning" alerts from the NWS.

4. Begin decision-making protocol at the first indication that weather conditions may affect the safety and operations of the school district.

5. Stage essential staff members and equipment, particularly school buses, in the event conditions warrant the closure of schools. Staging is critically important if the weather event is possible during the school day, because it can be difficult and time-consuming to call or recall bus drivers and buses to pick up students during the school day in the hectic

environment of an approaching storm. School buses should be readily available and quickly called to schools to transport students home.

Decision to Close Schools

1. The decision whether or not to close schools due to inclement weather is a very difficult decision because of numerous reasons, but primarily due to the unpredictability of weather conditions. That is why it is critically important to participate in NWS briefings and closely monitor updates and communicate frequently with local emergency management experts.

2. The difference between "Watch" and "Warning" is important at any time but is especially important when a decision to open or close schools has to be made.

3. It is prudent to assign staff members to different locations of the school district to monitor weather and road conditions. This is especially important in the early morning hours when a decision to open or close schools has to be made before school bus drivers begin their routes. If it is during the school day, local school administrators and other staff members should monitor weather and road conditions and report to the school district office. Also, contact local emergency management staff members, local law enforcement, and other local agencies such as the department of transportation to get updates on weather and road conditions.

4. Schools should have in place a decision protocol to determine if and when students should be released during potentially dangerous weather conditions. The decision should be based on the safety of the students. Sometimes it is unsafe to send students home walking, riding, or riding a school bus during a severe storm. However, if weather conditions are predicted to worsen, then the decision to release students would have to be weighed against that information.

5. Because transporting students home during the school day with hazardous weather and road conditions poses enormous challenges and risks, school districts schools should consider a preemptive closing of schools if a "Warning" has been issued.

6. Parents and the news media should be notified if schools close due to weather-related conditions. Announce closing on school district voice recording system for parents.

School Closing Before the School Day

1. Announce closing to school district staff members by use of school district phone tree, text messages, and email system.

2. Announce closing on school district voice recording system for parents and inform the news media using messaging system established by news media security system (news media outlets have a verification protocol to protect against bogus and unsubstantiated reports from school districts – typically by use of a code or password).

Closing School During the School Day

1. Announce closing to school district staff members by use of school district phone tree, text messages, and email system.

2. Announce closing on school district voice recording system for parents and inform the news media using messaging system established by news media security system.

3. Check on the condition of streets, roads, bridges, overpasses and surrounding neighborhoods to ensure that bus routes and routes for student walkers are clear.

4. Keep students who walk to and from school away from possible hazardous conditions, such as frozen or flooded

fields, sidewalks, pedestrian overpasses, etc. Contact their parents to pick them up at school.

5. Student dismissal procedures should remain as typical as possible, unless weather conditions are quickly worsening. Hasten the loading of buses by staging bus riders in groups as assigned by bus routes, so that the buses can quickly load the students. If the weather conditions are unsafe for student walkers, hold the students in the classrooms until their parents arrive.

6. Crisis Management Team should ensure that all students have left the school.

7. Crisis Management Team should ensure that all other staff members have left the school.

8. Crisis Management Team should secure the school.

Shelter-in-Place Protocol

If weather conditions create the necessity for overnight housing of students and staff members at the school, the school must be secured and student movement limited and monitored.

Preparation for Shelter-in-Place:

Each school should be prepared for shelter-in-place by planning for such an event, because depending on conditions, it may be too late to secure essential elements for sheltering after the event occurs. Access to food, water, first-aid, sleeping areas, blankets, and communications are absolutely essential. Climate control of the school is important, so predetermined measures should be in place to provide heating or cooling, as needed. Staff member assignments should be predetermined, discussed and practiced. Plans should include a protocol for securing the school, accounting at all times for students and staff members, communicating with parents, and meeting the physical and emotional needs of students and staff members. It can be very difficult to shelter in students, due to their high levels of anxiety and fear, and it is equally difficult to comfort them physically and emotionally. Trying to provide food and water will be complex unless a plan was previously developed for sheltering. Even though the Crisis Management Team will coordinate the sheltering protocol, the role and support of each school staff member is critical.

Precautions are necessary when the sheltering in place ends, because parents and students will be so anxious to reunite. This can create security problems to account for each student and ensure that they are released safely to parents. Plans for searching the school to make certain all students are accounted for and have left the school must be developed. The plans should also include a protocol for securing the school and assessing damage or resource depletion once the sheltering event has ended. The plans should include a protocol for evaluating the school before students and staff members return for normal operations following the event.

Response to Shelter-in-Place

1. The decision to provide overnight housing will be a joint decision between the school administrative staff members,

school district office staff members, and emergency personnel.

2. When the decision is made to have overnight housing, the school's administrative staff members will contact the school district office and the news media will be informed by the school district office.

3. If the HVAC and other systems are centralized, the school's administrative staff members should contact the *School district service center* to ensure that the school's climate control system is **not** turned off.

4. Designated school staff members will help contact family members and will continue to do so throughout the night.

5. Students and staff members will be routed to the safest part of the school and secured.

6. The administrative staff members and other staff members will be assigned supervision duties and shifts and will set up an indoor security perimeter to ensure the safety and supervision of the students. Also, shifts to answer the phones or respond to other means of communications will be established.

7. Roll should be taken periodically throughout the sheltering event to account for every student and staff member, and appropriate next day (or release day) checkout procedures should be followed to ensure the safe release of students.

8. Protocol to ensure that all students have left the school should be followed.

9. Contact School district service center to inspect school for possible damage and to determine what resources need to be restocked in the school.

10. School district office should determine when the school is ready to resume normal operations and announce to the news media and parents.

11. Administrative staff members, with assistance from the School System Information Office, should prepare a written statement to be sent home with students.

Death of a Staff Member or Student Protocol

Administrative staff members should respond quickly to news of the death of a student or staff members. Students and staff members will turn to and rely on leadership of the school to respond appropriately to this type of crisis that can evoke strong emotions.

1. Contact Crisis Management Team

2. Contact the school district office

3. Crisis Management Team, administrative staff members and counseling staff members should begin informing staff members and students, without providing details of the cause or circumstances of the death.

4. Designate locations in the school for students who may need individual or small group sessions for grieving.

5. Designate locations in the school for staff members who may need individual or small group sessions for grieving.

6. Administrative staff members and the Crisis Management Team should prepare a written statement to be sent home with students, without providing details of the cause or circumstances of the death or the name of the student or staff members member.

Suicide or Suicide Attempt at School Protocol

1. Call 911 where available or call emergency services.

2. Activate the school's Crisis Management Team.

3. Call school district office.

4. Clear the area around the affected student or staff members member

5. Limit activity in the vicinity of the affected student or staff members member and relocate students and staff members as necessary.

6. Assign staff members to make certain the school parking lot area is clear so first responders can reach the school with equipment.

7. Assign staff members to stand outside of the school to receive first responders in order to direct them to the student or staff member.

8. Send notes and runners to staff members informing them that a medical emergency has occurred or use the school's communication system. Include any additional instructions (e.g., "The bell schedule will be changed and will be manually sounded at an appropriate time.")

9. Designate locations in the school for students who may need individual or small group sessions for grieving.

10. Designate locations in the school for staff members who may need individual or small group sessions for grieving.

11. Administrative staff members and the Crisis Management Team should prepare a written statement to be sent home with students, without providing details of the incident or the name of the student or staff members.

NOTE: If a student threatens suicide, the counseling and administrative offices must be informed immediately. Also, the Crisis Management Team must be contacted as soon as possible. The student should be taken to the counseling office and someone should remain with the student at all times until the parents, the Crisis Management Team and first responders arrive.

Fire or Smoke in the School Protocol

A fire or smoke in a school requires immediate evacuation of the school. Even if smoke is confined to one part of the school, the school should be evacuated. Fire and smoke are very unpredictable and can spread exceedingly fast. A safe, orderly evacuation depends on effective fire drill practices.

1. Activate fire alarm system.

2. Call 911 where available or call emergency services.

3. Use intercom to start the evacuation.

4. Activate the school's Crisis Management Team.

5. Staff members and students should move to the predetermined assembly points 1,000 feet away from the school using predetermined routes and exits (**NOTE**: administrators must re-direct classes if the predetermined routes pass near the fire or smoke areas.)

6. Ensure that all staff members and students have left the school. Check hallways, restrooms, lounges, cafeterias, auditoriums, and gymnasiums.

7. Designated staff members should take the Emergency Kit to the evacuation site(s).

8. Use walkie/talkies, cell phones, bullhorns and adult runners to communicate and confirm that the school has been cleared.

9. Designated staff members should account for all students by checking with teachers in the evacuation site (s).

10. Designated staff members should survey students at the assembly point (s) to check for injuries or trauma.

11. If the school has to be evacuated away from the school campus use the "card" system, which includes giving all

teachers three color-coded cards: Green Card-all students are present; Yellow Card-students are missing but the teacher knows where they can be found; Red Card-teacher needs immediate assistance.

12. Assign staff members at the evacuation site to collect critical information and to manage and monitor students at the assembly site(s).

13. School administrators should collect lists of unaccounted for students from staff members and compare with the daily attendance absentee list and notify first responders of missing students.

14. Identify the location of classes in the evacuation site(s) to facilitate an orderly transfer of students to their parents.

15. Direct parents to the assembly site(s) to pick up students. The news media can be used to inform parents of the situation and that they may pick their students up at the assembly site or wait for them to be brought home via school bus. This will be determined based on circumstances.

16. Set up a sign-out area at the assembly site(s) and release students only to pre-determined authorized persons using the sign-out procedure.

17. Instruct parents or guardians to leave the site to make room for others once they have signed out their student.

18. As conditions allow, monitor the assembly site so students can begin loading unto buses, and a manifest should be established to account for all students riding buses.

19. Students not riding buses and not picked up by parents or guardians should remain in the evacuation site(s) until an authorized person arrives to pick them up.

20. Maintain contact with police/fire department(s) to stay informed about conditions at the school site.

21. All staff members and students must remain in the evacuation site until the "all clear" signal is sent.

22. Call school district office.

23. Contact school district service center to inspect school for possible damage.

24. Administrative staff members, with assistance from the School System Information Office and/or the Crisis Management Team, should prepare a written statement to be sent home with students.

Most states require that at least one fire drill be conducted each month when school is in session. Some states permit schools to substitute a severe weather drill for its required monthly fire drill during the months of February and November.

Hazardous Materials (Chemical/Biological/Nuclear Threat or

Accident) **Protocol**

There are numerous possible hazardous material threats to schools. Most of the threats are created by unsafe use of chemicals at school by students or staff members. Also, some schools are near industrial parks that contain above-ground chemical storage tanks while other schools are within a mile of interstate highways or railroad tracks where hazardous material is hauled and where accidental spills may occur. Some hazardous materials are immediately toxic when breached from containers, with toxic fumes, for example. Schools that are within one mile of interstate highways, railroad tracks, underground or above ground pipelines, or chemical or petroleum storage tanks should identify the risks and have protocols in place for a rapid evacuation of the school and area.

Preparation

1. Make a risk assessment of potentially hazardous materials which are in the vicinity of the school. Note the location and affected routes that may be sealed off or dangerous in the event of a spill and designate alternate routes for the evacuation.

2. If the school is near a potential source of hazardous material release, the school should develop a rapid evacuation protocol, which requires having immediate access to school bus drivers and school buses.

3. All schools should have weather monitors, but schools near potential hazardous material spills should have monitors that include warnings of hazardous material spills in addition to weather information. The monitor should be located in the school where staff members can listen for alerts at all times.

Hazardous Materials Accident in School Protocol

High school chemistry laboratories should be inspected several times during the school year to ensure that chemicals are used, stored, and accounted for correctly. Each high school should have a Chemical Hygiene Plan and updated Material Safety Data Sheet (MSDS). All chemicals must be labeled and properly handled. There should be a chemical shelf storage pattern for inorganics and organics, and a plan for storage, maintenance and handling of compressed gas cylinders. Also, each school should have a chemical disposal protocol.

Response

1. Call 911 where available or call emergency services.

2. Immediately remove all students and staff members from the area.

3. **DO NOT TOUCH THE HAZARDOUS MATERIAL.**

4. Alert the school's Crisis Management Team.

5. Seal off the area (s) around and near the accident.

6. Shut down air-conditioning and ventilation units or contact the school district service center to do so to prevent any toxic fumes from entering the system.

7. Evacuate students and staff members to a predetermined assembly points 1,000 feet away from the school using predetermined routes and exits (**NOTE**: administrators must re-direct classes if the predetermined routes pass near the hazardous material accident site).

8. Ensure that all staff members and students have left the school. Check hallways, restrooms, lounges, cafeterias, auditoriums, and gymnasiums.

9. Designated staff members should take the Emergency Kit to the evacuation site(s).

10. Use walkie/talkies, cell phones, bullhorns and adult runners to communicate and confirm that the school has been cleared.

11. If the school has to be evacuated away from the school campus use the "card" system, which includes giving all teachers three color-coded cards: Green Card-all students are present; Yellow Card-students are missing but the teacher knows where they can be found; Red Card-teacher needs immediate assistance.

12. Assign staff members at the evacuation site to collect critical information and to manage and monitor students at the assembly site(s).

13. School administrators should collect lists of unaccounted for students from staff members and compare with the daily attendance absentee list and notify first responders of missing students.

14. Identify the location of classes in the evacuation site(s) to facilitate an orderly transfer of students to their parents.

15. Direct parents to the assembly site(s) to pick up students. The news media can be used to inform parents of the situation and that they may pick their students up at the assembly site or wait for them to be brought home via school bus. This will be determined based on circumstances.

16. Set up a sign-out area at the assembly site(s) and release students only to pre-determined authorized persons using the sign-out procedure.

17. Instruct parents or guardians to leave the site to make room for others once they have signed out their student.

18. As conditions allow, monitor the assembly site so students can begin loading unto buses, and a manifest should be established to account for all students riding buses.

19. Students not riding buses and not picked up by parents or guardians should remain in the evacuation site(s) until an authorized person arrives to pick them up.

20. Maintain contact with police/fire department(s) to stay informed about conditions at the school site.

21. Designated staff members should account for all students by checking with teachers in the evacuation site(s).

22. Designated staff members should survey students at the assembly point to check for injuries or trauma.

23. All staff members and students must remain in the evacuation site until the "all clear" signal is sent.

24. Call school district office.

25. Contact school district service center to inspect school for possible damage.

26. Ensure that the school has been cleared before students and staff members return to school.

27. Administrative staff members, with assistance from the School System Information Office and/or the Crisis Management Team, should prepare a written statement to be sent home with students.

Hazardous Materials Accident Outside of School Protocol

Schools usually receive notice from emergency personnel of hazardous material accidents or threats originating outside of the school. Typically, the local emergency management agency or local fire and rescue will notify the school of the situation and risks. If the notice comes from *non-emergency sources*, the school administrative staff members should contact **911,** local emergency management or local fire and rescue to confirm or refute the report. If the notice comes from emergency sources, the emergency management agency and/or fire and rescue will control the situation and indicate if the school should be evacuated. It will aid them if the following procedures are immediately initiated.

1. Alert the school's Crisis Management Team.

2. Return all students and staff members from athletic fields, gyms, playground and other areas into the school.

3. Assign designated staff members to ensure that students and staff members do not leave the school.

4. Contact school district transportation to keep school buses out of the hazardous material accident/threat area that may be on field trips or at other school-sponsored events and either take students to predetermined evacuation sites or return to school. Depending on the nature of the incident and location, school bus drivers should be alerted to standby for possible evacuation of the school. Since a hazardous material situation can be unstable and present an immediate danger, all school bus drivers throughout the school district should be alerted and on standby to quickly go to the school or schools for an expedited evacuation.

5. Use intercom to inform students and staff members that precautionary measures are being taken due to a report of a hazardous materials accident in the community

6. Instruct all students and staff members to return to their classroom, work areas, or assigned support areas.

7. Teachers should make sure all students are accounted for and immediately report any missing students to school administrators.

8. Close all windows and outside doors to the school.

9. Ask local emergency management agency or fire and rescue if the school's air-conditioning and ventilation units should be shut down. If affirmed, immediately deactivate all ventilation and air-conditioning systems or contact the school district service center to do so and prepare to move students away from windows and doors.

10. Call school district office to report the situation.

11. Be prepared to quickly evacuate the facility, based on the directions of local emergency management or fire and rescue.

12. Have first aid trained staff members on alert.

13. Remain in lockdown mode until the "all clear" signal/message is received from local emergency management agency or fire and rescue or unless an evacuation is ordered.

14. Use intercom to inform students and staff members of the "all clear" signal/message and to give a brief explanation of the reason for the lockdown response or to announce the evacuation procedures, if required.

15. If an evacuation is ordered in a hazardous material situation, expect local law enforcement to manage the flow of traffic and even escort the school buses out of the area. It is imperative to follow the instructions of local emergency management, fire and rescue and law enforcement to ensure that the school buses are not traveling toward the hazard.

16. If the school has to be evacuated away from the school campus use the "card" system, which includes giving all teachers three color-coded cards: Green Card-all students are present; Yellow Card-students are missing but the teacher knows where they can be found; Red Card-teacher needs immediate assistance.

17. Assign staff members at the evacuation site to collect critical information and to manage and monitor students at the assembly site(s).

18. School administrators should collect lists of unaccounted for students from staff members and compare with the daily attendance absentee list and notify first responders of missing students.

19. Identify the location of classes in the evacuation site(s) to facilitate an orderly transfer of students to their parents.

20. Direct parents to the assembly site(s) to pick up students. The news media can be used to inform parents of the situation and that they may pick their students up at the assembly site or wait for them to be brought home via school bus. This will be determined based on circumstances.

21. Set up a sign-out area at the assembly site(s) and release students only to pre-determined authorized persons using the sign-out procedure.

22. Instruct parents or guardians to leave the site to make room for others once they have signed out their student.

23. As conditions allow, monitor the assembly site so students can begin loading unto buses, and a manifest should be established to account for all students riding buses.

24. Students not riding buses and not picked up by parents or guardians should remain in the evacuation site(s) until an authorized person arrives to pick them up.

25. Maintain contact with police/fire department(s) to stay informed about conditions at the school site.

26. Administrative staff members, with assistance from the School System Information Office and/or the Crisis Management Team, should prepare a written statement to be sent home with students.

Report of a Weapon on Campus Protocol

The report of a weapon on campus requires immediate action, based on the information in the report. It is important to ascertain the type and location of the weapon as soon as possible.

Response

1. Immediately inform the School Resource Officer and Call 911 where available or call emergency services and law enforcement and lockdown the school.

2. Administrator and School Resource Officer (or other law enforcement officer) should proceed to the classroom or area where the weapon may be located.

3. If a student is suspected of possessing a weapon, the School Resource Officer and an administrator should escort the suspected student (or person) to a secured location and another administrator or designated staff members member should carry all of the student's belongings at a safe distance.

4. The student should always walk in front of the escort; never allow the student to walk behind any member of the escort.

5. At no time should the student be allowed to put his/her hands in pockets or to approach his/her belongings, nor should the student be allowed to go to a classroom or restroom while on the way to the secured location.

6. After reaching the secured location the student should be searched following established procedures dictated by local board policy and local law enforcement standards.

7. The student or person's belongings should be thoroughly searched following established procedures dictated by local board policy and local law enforcement standards.

8. Any weapon found should be immediately secured. If found by an administrator or teacher or other staff members member, the weapon must be turned over to the police. **STAFF MEMBERS SHOULD NEVER ATTEMPT TO UNLOAD A FIREARM.**

9. At least two administrators or staff members should search the student's locker, following established procedures dictated by local board policy.

10. If a weapon is found in the locker, the area should be secured and a law enforcement officer should remove the weapon.

11. Administrators or school staff members should not confront or attempt to disarm anyone who is in possession of a weapon.

12. Assign staff members to make certain the school parking lot area is clear so first responders can reach the school with equipment.

13. Assign staff members to stand outside of the school to receive first responders in order to direct them to the student or staff member.

14. Remain on lockdown until the "all clear" signal is given.

15. Administrative staff members, with assistance from the School System Information Office and/or the Crisis Management Team, should prepare a written statement to be sent home with students.

NOTE: If the suspected person is in a classroom or other crowded area, the approach to the student should be carefully planned. If the person runs, he/she should not be chased. Secure the school and allow local law enforcement to pursue the person.

When Firearm Shots are Heard on or Near School Campus Protocol

1. Call 911 where available or call emergency services and local law enforcement.

2. Immediately lockdown the school – bring all students into the school; clear hallways, cafeteria, restrooms, gym, locker room and any other area or room that cannot be locked.

3. Contact staff members outdoors with students to take refuge in a predetermined site if returning to the school is unsafe.

4. View surveillance monitor and to determine location and nature of the incident.

5. Remain on lockdown until the "all clear" signal is given.

6. Administrative staff members, with assistance from the School System Information Office and/or the Crisis Management Team, should prepare a written statement to be sent home with students.

Active Shooter in School Protocol

At the first report or other indication of an active shooter on campus, immediately lockdown the school unless escaping the school is possible and safe. The United States Department of Homeland Security recommends the following in response to an active shooter on campus or in the school.

First Response – Flee the Situation

1. Be aware of the environment and any possible dangers.

2. Have an escape route and plan in mind.

3. Take note of the two nearest exits in any facility being visit.

4. If in an office, stay there and secure the door.

5. If in a hallway, get into a room and secure the door.

6. Evacuate regardless of whether others agree to follow.

7. Leave belongings behind.

8. Help others escape, if possible.

9. Prevent individuals from entering an area where the active shooter may be.

10. Keep hands visible in case law enforcement is in the area.

11. Follow the instructions of any police officers.

If Evacuation is Not Possible, Hide Out

- If evacuation is not possible, find a place to hide where the active shooter is less likely to find you.
-
    Hiding place should:

1. Be out of the active shooter's view.

2. Provide protection if shots are fired in your direction (i.e., an office with a closed and locked door).

3. Not trap or restrict options for movement.

- To prevent an active shooter from entering hiding place:

  1. Lock the door.

  2. Blockade the door with heavy furniture.

- If the active shooter is nearby:

  1. Lock the door.

  2. Silence cell phone and/or pager.

  3. Turn off any source of noise (i.e., radios, televisions).

  4. Hide behind large items (i.e., cabinets, desks).

  5. Remain quiet.

If Evacuation or Hiding are Not Possible Take Action Against the Active Shooter

- As a last resort, and only when in imminent danger, attempt to disrupt and/or incapacitate the active shooter:

  1. Act as aggressively as possible against him/her – punch, hit, kick, scratch, etc.

  2. Throw items and improvise using anything available as a weapon

3.   Yell and scream

NOTE: Remain on lockdown or on evacuation status until the "all clear" signal is given.   Administrative staff members, with assistance from the School System Information Office and/or the Crisis Management Team, should prepare a written statement to be sent home with students.

Intruder or Suspicious Person Protocol

An intruder or suspicious person is someone whose presence is uninvited and unwelcome and/or whose behavior jeopardizes the safety of the school. An intruder or suspicious person situation may escalate into a hostage or barricade emergency.

Preparation

Being prepared often discourages outsiders from attempting to intrude upon the school environment.

1. Restrict free access to the school to as few doors as possible and ensure that all doors are either secured or monitored at all times.

2. All exterior doors locked during the day should have signs that provide directions to visitors advising them to use the main entrance.

3. Discourage students and staff members from opening locked doors for others, because this will breach school security.

4. Schools should use a visitor identification name-tag system. Visitor tags should be disposable.

5. Designate a school employee to periodically check all exterior doors that have been designated as secured doors.

Response

1. When a lockdown is necessary to protect students and staff members, it is essential that the lockdown take place immediately – delaying a lockdown may be dangerous.

2. When a lockdown is deemed necessary, use the intercom system to announce school-wide lockdown.

3. Call 911 where available or call emergency services and local law enforcement.

4. Alert the school's Crisis Management Team.

5. Make sure the hallways are clear of students and staff members.

6. Use walkie/talkie to inform teachers on the athletic fields or playground to stay away from the school.

7. Be prepared to seek protection in a nearby room if the intruder or suspicious person approaches the school or grounds.

8. Monitor the location of the intruder or suspicious person using the surveillance cameras and monitors and walkie/talkies.

9. Allow no one to leave the classrooms.

10. Close all windows and blinds.

11. Encourage students to remain calm and quiet.

12. Remain in lockdown mode until the "all clear" signal/message is received.

13. Call school district office.

14. Administrative staff members, with assistance from the School System Information Office and/or the Crisis Management Team, should prepare a written statement to be sent home with students.

Hostage or Barricade Situation Protocol

(Staff members <u>SHOULD NOT</u> attempt to negotiate with a hostage taker.)

1. Call 911 where available or call emergency services and local law enforcement.

2. Immediately lockdown the school.

3. Make sure the hallways, restrooms, gyms, and cafeteria are clear of students and staff members.

4. Use walkie/talkie to inform teachers on the athletic fields or playground to stay away from the school.

5. Use the intercom system to announce school-wide lockdown.

6. Be prepared to initiate evacuation procedures.

7. Have first aid trained staff members on alert.

8. Remain in lockdown mode until further communications from school staff members or emergency management agency or local law enforcement staff members.

Evacuation

1. Staff members and students move to the predetermined assembly points 1,000 feet away from the school using predetermined routes and exits (**NOTE**: administrators must re-direct classes if the predetermined routes pass near the hostage/barricade area.)

2. Ensure that all staff members and students have left the school. Check hallways, restrooms, lounges, cafeterias, auditoriums, and gymnasiums.

3. Designated staff members should take the Crisis Emergency Kit to the evacuation site (s).

4. Use walkie/talkies, cell phones, bullhorns and adult runners to communicate and confirm that the school has been cleared.

5. Designated staff members should account for all students by checking with teachers in the evacuation site (s).

6. Designated staff members should survey students at the assembly point to check for injuries or trauma.

7. Everyone should remain in evacuation sites until the "all clear" signal/message is given. Once students are in the school, use intercom to explain situation.

8. Administrative staff members, with assistance from the School System Information Office and/or the Crisis Management Team, should prepare a written statement to be sent home with students.

Student Disruption or Civil Disturbances Protocol

Student disruptions of a large scale almost always start as seemingly insignificant disagreements; therefore, student disruptions involving even a few students should be quickly handled before the situation escalates.

Level 1 Disturbance - Disruption is confined to one area, but no threat to students or staff members.

Level 2 Disturbance - Disruption forces are mobile and may pose a threat to students and/or staff members.

Level 3 Disturbance – Disruption is widespread with large-scale student participation and is a serious threat to students and staff members.

For Level 2 and Level 3 Disturbances:

1. Immediately lockdown the school.

2. Call 911 or emergency services and local law enforcement.

3. Alert the school's Crisis Management Team.

4. Use intercom system to signal level and location of disturbance (e.g., "We have a Level 3 in third hall) and specific instructions.

5. Isolate the disruption.

6. Clear the immediate area, including restrooms and hallways.

7. Use walkie/talkies to monitor and assess the situation in order to provide instructions for staff members.

8. Staff members trained in CPR and First Aid should go to the area (if they are supervising students, a staff members member should be designated to relieve them when they move to the area).

9. Assign staff members to make certain the school parking lot area is clear so first responders can reach the school with equipment.

10. Assign staff members to stand outside of the school to receive first responders in order to direct them to the student or staff member.

Additional Notes:

1. Teachers should not leave students unsupervised.

2. Staff members should not approach the disturbance area alone.

3. Staff members should clearly and loudly communicate simple instructions to students involved in the disturbance.

4. When approaching a crowd, remove the crowd one "layer" at a time from the outside in; do not push through the crowd toward the center or point of the disruption.

5. If the disturbance is too large or too outrageous to intervene, wait for law enforcement to arrive and in the meantime attempt to control and direct students on the outside of the disruption and prevents others from entering the disruption.

6. Do not allow students removed from the disturbance area access to lockers.

7. Use intercom to inform students and staff members of the "all clear" signal/message and to give a brief explanation of the reason for the lockdown response.

8. Plan close supervision of students during dismissal and boarding of buses. Coordinate with law enforcement to ensure adequate protection of students until they have left the premises.

9. Contact School district service center to inspect school for possible damage.

10. Call school district office

11. Administrative staff members, with assistance from the School System Information Office and/or the Crisis Management Team, should prepare a written statement to be sent home with students.

12. Provide extra security and/or administrators for the next several days following the disturbance to dissuade retaliation.

Student Runaways/Student Abduction/Missing Student Protocol

There are few things more important than a school's ability to locate any student at any time for virtually any reason.

Preparation

Ensure that student accountability procedures are in place and strictly followed at all times:

1. Daily attendance kept and parents notified of absences.

2. Daily tardies recorded and parents notified.

3. Field-trip student rosters are kept on each bus and a copy at the school.

4. At field-trip destination, all students are accounted for upon arrival and prior to departure.

5. Emergency medical information should be up-to-date.

6. Emergency contact numbers should be up-to-date.

7. Parent contact information should be up-to-date.

8. Enforce identification and accountability procedures for anyone who enters the school while the school is in session.

9. Ensure that procedures are followed when releasing students to parents or other authorized adult.

Response

1. Lockdown the school immediately.

2. Alert the school's Crisis Management Team.

3. Call 911 where available or call emergency services and law enforcement.

4. Have the name, description, picture of the missing student and parent contact information ready to give law enforcement.

5. Notify the parents/guardians.

6. Notify transportation if the student normally rides the bus.

7. Conduct a room-by-room search for the student. Also, search grounds and other potential hiding areas.

8. Survey students from the missing student's class for information about the missing student.

9. Siblings of the missing student should be closely monitored at all times. If the siblings attend a different school, the administrator of that facility should be notified <u>immediately</u>.

10. Secure the perimeter of the school. Make sure students do not leave.

11. Curtail outside activities until the situation has stabilized.

12. Assign staff members to make certain the school parking lot area is clear so first responders can reach the school with equipment.

13. Assign staff members to stand outside of the school to receive first responders in order to direct them to the student or staff member.

14. Call school district office.

15. Administrative staff members, with assistance from the School System Information Office and/or the Crisis Management Team, should prepare a written statement to be sent home with students.

16. Provide extra security and/or administrators for the next several days following the incident.

Nature-Related Crisis Protocols: Tornado, Flooding, Earthquake,

Hurricane

Certain areas of the country are more susceptible than others to nature-related conditions such as blizzards, hurricanes, and flooding. However, a natural disaster is possible anywhere in the country, even in previously unaffected areas. Therefore, schools have to be prepared for unpredictable natural disasters.

Tornado and Tornado-Like Conditions Protocol

Definitions

- **Tornado WATCH:** Indicates that weather conditions are present that **may** develop into a tornado. Move students from all mobile classrooms to the main school.

- **Tornado WARNING:** Indicates that a tornado has been sighted in the immediate area. Protective measures must be taken immediately, starting with moving students from all mobile classrooms to the main school.

Preparedness

1. Evaluate the physical plant, and develop plans for the use of secure areas by student and staff members. CLEARLY identify the areas for all staff members.

2. Plan for the use of lower floors and/or interior areas such as hallways.

3. Do not use gyms and other areas with wide roof spans.

4. Inform staff members and students what signal means a **Tornado WARNING** (it is imperative that students and staff members know the signal for a tornado warning).

5. Keep First Aid supplies current and convenient.

6. At least twice a year, inform staff members and students about severe weather and the appropriate response.

7. Designate the best areas to serve as shelters, such as interior rooms, hallways, lowest floors, enclosed smaller areas away from glass, etc.

8. Prepare diagrams of the school, and mark the tornado shelter areas thereon. Include the quickest route to access those shelters, and post the diagrams in each room.

9. Conduct drills/exercises so that everyone knows tornado warning procedures.

10. Designate staff members to monitor weather reports on the radio.

Response to Tornado WARNING

1. Move students from all temporary or mobile classrooms to the main school (multi-purpose schools do not provide safe shelter during severe storms).

2. Take personal belongings only to provide extra protection from flying or falling debris (e.g., notebooks or coats to hold over head and shoulders).

3. Alert the school's Crisis Management Team.

4. Secure the school by closing windows and doors.

5. Direct everyone to seek cover in the hallways and to take a protective seated position with hands/arms covering the head, neck and face.

6. If possible, secure or store articles that may become missiles indoors.

7. Students in unsafe locations should go to a pre-determined location; for example, from classrooms with windows into the hallway (Note: if the hallways have skylights students should be relocated to another part of the school.)

8. Students should not be allowed to leave the school during a **WARNING**.

9. If students are on a field trip at the time inclement weather occurs, bus drivers should be alerted to get students back on the bus and return to school or a safe haven.

10. Teachers should keep their class rosters with them during the drill and remain with the class to be sure all students are present and are taking safety precautions.

11. The National Weather Service recommends that schools not release students at dismissal time if a severe storm is in the immediate area unless there are predictions that the storm will worsen and conditions will deteriorate even more. In these situations a decision will need to be made whether to dismiss students or shelter-in-place short-term or long-term. Sometimes the situation only requires delaying the bus riders and walkers until the storm has passed.

12. Staff members trained in CPR and First Aid should be assigned to the sheltered areas.

13. Call 911 or emergency services if students or staff members are injured.

14. Assign staff members to make certain the school parking lot area is clear so first responders can reach the school with equipment.

15. Assign staff members to stand outside of the school to receive first responders in order to direct them to the student or staff member.

16. Students and teachers should remain in the secured areas and safety positions until the "all clear" signal is given.

17. Contact School district service center to inspect school for damage.

18. Administrative staff members, with assistance from the School System Information Office and/or the Crisis Management Team, should prepare a written statement to be sent home with students.

Additional Notes

1. If the storm causes damage to the school, student and staff members movement in the school following the storm should be closely monitored to identify unsafe parts of the school. Also, if the school day ends early due to the storm, activate the early dismissal procedures. If parents come to the school to check on and to check out their children, set up an orderly check out procedure in the school cafeteria area (if safe), requiring identification and using student attendance logs.

2. If the storm damaged the school, the decision to open or close the school the next school day and subsequent days should be made jointly by the following only after a school building inspector has determined that the school structure is safe to reenter.

   o Superintendent's office
   o Principal and staff members
   o Law enforcement
   o Local County Emergency Personnel

3. The school district office should inform the local news media to announce the decision to open or close the school to the public.

Severe Thunderstorm Warning

1. Move students from all temporary or mobile classrooms to the main school (multi-purpose schools to not provide safe shelter during severe weather).

2. Bring all students into the school from outside activities and keep students from leaving the school until the warning is cancelled.

3. Where possible, all electronic equipment should be unplugged.

4. Keep students and staff members away from glassed areas.

5. The National Weather Service recommends that schools not release students at dismissal time if a severe storm is in the immediate area unless there are predictions that the storm will worsen and conditions will deteriorate even more. In these situations a decision will need to be made whether to dismiss students or shelter-in-place.

6. Closely monitor weather developments and announcements.

Flooding Protocol

According to the 30-year average calculated by FEMA, no other natural disaster has taken more lives each year than flooding. It only takes six inches of moving water to knock a person off their feet and carry them away. It should also be noted that flooding can occur in areas without a history of floods when it is exposed to torrential rain. That is why it is important for all schools to consider the possibility of flooding. Flood alerts, including Flash Flood alerts, are announced on Digital Weather Alert Monitors. Schools in communities with a history of flooding should be alert to rain conditions and rain forecasts.

Preparedness

1. Know the local history of flooding near the school and in the community.

2. Know what a river, stream, or lake height (flood stage) forecast means in terms of the school, community, bus routes and student residential areas.

3. Know local elevations.

4. Plan alternative transportation routes to avoid flood-prone areas.

5. Make provisions for students living in flood affected areas to be taken home early, kept at school, or taken to relatives.

Response

1. Monitor weather conditions in the affected areas via radio or television broadcasts.

2. Evacuate students immediately in accordance with emergency early dismissal procedures and with assistance from local law enforcement and emergency management agency.

3. Contact school district office to issue news release regarding early dismissal.

4. Closely monitor dismissal to keep students away from flooded, flooding, or possible flooding areas.

5. Warn students walking home from school to stay away from creeks, rivers, stream, lakes, dams, and any flooding areas or areas with flash flood potential.

6. If the situation does not permit dismissal due to flooding conditions, keep the students at school or in an alternate safe location, based on instructions from emergency management agency or law enforcement.

7. If flood waters endanger the school's water supply, shut off the water at mains so that contaminated water will not back up into the school water supply.

8. If the flooding damaged the school, the decision to open or close the school the next school day and subsequent days should be made jointly by the following only after a school building inspector has determined that the school structure is safe to reenter.

   ✓ Superintendent's office

   ✓ Principal and staff members

   ✓ Law enforcement

   ✓ Local County Emergency Personnel

9. The school district office should inform the local news media to announce the decision to open or close the school to the public.

If flood waters approaches the school or if a flash flood warning area includes the school:

1. Students and staff members should be relocated from low-lying levels and all electrical equipment should be unplugged.

2. If flooding can or does damage to the school or make areas of the school unsafe or potentially unsafe, student and staff member should be moved immediately to predesignated areas of the school that can be supervised and from which a quick evacuation is possible. Do not put students and staff members in an area of the school that can be sealed off by rising water.

3. If parents come to the school to check on and to check out their children, set up an orderly check out procedure, requiring identification and using student attendance logs.

4. If the flooding damaged the school, the decision to open or close the school the next school day and subsequent days should be made jointly by the following only after a school building inspector has determined that the school structure is safe to reenter.

   ✓ Superintendent's office

   ✓ Principal and staff members

   ✓ Law enforcement

   ✓ Local County Emergency Personnel

5. The school district office should inform the local news media to announce the decision to open or close the school to the public.

Hurricane and Hurricane-Like Conditions Protocol

Preparedness

1. Monitor weather reports and assign members of the school's Crisis Management Team to receive calls from emergency personnel, school district office, state emergency management agency, and/or the National Weather Service.

2. Secure any equipment that may become a projectile during the storm.

3. Unplug all electrical equipment.

4. Remove or secure all objects, equipment, and materials that may fall to the floor.

5. Contact the School district service center and the local emergency management agency or the state emergency management agency for more information on school preparations.

6. If the school has been designated as an evacuation shelter, determine its readiness to receive citizens.

7. With the assistance of local emergency management agency or the state emergency management agency identify and designate the most appropriate protective areas within the school.

8. Work with the local emergency management agency or the state emergency management agency to develop a plan to provide provisions for temporary shelter and for checking-in and checking-out evacuees.

9. Check school activity calendar to identify school activities or events that conflict within the estimated time period for the hurricane warning area. Reschedule those activities in time to announce to students, staff members, and public.

Response

In most situations involving a hurricane, ample time will be available to make long-range plans for school, including closing schools until the storm has passed, so the emphasis will shift to recovery.

1. If flood waters endangered the school's water supply, shut off the water at mains so that contaminated water will not back up into the school water supply.

2. If the flooding damaged the school, the decision to open or close the school the next school day and subsequent days should be made jointly by the following only after a school building inspector has determined that the school structure is safe to reenter.

   ✓ Superintendent's office
   ✓ Principal and staff members
   ✓ Law enforcement
   ✓ Local County Emergency Personnel

3. The school district office should inform the local news media to announce the decision to open or close the school to the public.

Earthquake (Seismic Activity) Protocol

In any geographic area, three main factors together determine seismic risks: the level of seismic hazard, the number of people and amount of property that are exposed to seismic hazards and how vulnerable people and property are to the hazards. Seismic hazard levels differ significantly across the United States, both between and within states. The Federal Emergency Management Agency (FEMA) Earthquake Hazard Maps at *fema.gov* provides maps and levels of risks for the entire country. These and other maps that depict earthquake and seismic hazard levels throughout the country are produced by the U.S. Geological Survey (USGS). For more maps and related information, visit the USGS Earthquake Hazards Program website. Information about seismic hazards in high risk parts of the nation is available from regional earthquake consortia affiliated with FEMA. Seismic hazards in the central United States, home of the New Madrid Seismic Zone, are tracked by the Central United States Earthquake Consortium; those in many western states by the Western States Seismic Policy Council; those in the Pacific Northwest by the Cascadia Region Earthquake Workgroup and those in northeastern states by the Northeast States Emergency Consortium.

Preparation

After reviewing the level of risk, plan accordingly. It is difficult to plan evacuation routes and reunification cites because of the unpredictability of seismic activity and earthquakes. However, FEMA recommends that planning for seismic activity and earthquake include the following:

1. Check with local building-regulatory agency to find out whether the school is subject to building codes containing seismic design provisions.

2. Anchor nonstructural items that are not braced, reinforced, or otherwise secured.

3. If schools are in a Moderate to High Risk Level earthquake area students and staff members should be trained to respond to the event.

Response

1. Movement during the tremors is not recommended.

2. Staff members and students inside the school should take cover under desks, when possible, and cover their heads and necks. They should stay away from glass, outside windows and doors, shelves, and any objects that may fall. Students and staff members in classrooms with windows should relocate to the hallways or stairwells. Students or staff members in wheelchairs should lock the wheels and remain seated until the event ends. Pillows or books should be available for students and staff members to use, especially for those in wheelchairs, to cover their heads and necks if desks and tables are not available.

3. Staff members and students outside the school should move away from the school and avoid utility lines.

After the Seismic Activity Stops

1. Alert the school's Crisis Management.

2. If there is damage or potential damage to the school, staff members and students should move to a predetermined assembly points 1,000 feet away from the school using predetermined routes and exits (**NOTE**: administrators must re-direct classes if the predetermined routes pass near damaged areas.)

3. Ensure that all staff members and students have left the school. Check hallways, restrooms, lounges, cafeterias, auditoriums, and gymnasiums.

4. Designated staff members should take the Crisis Emergency Kit to the evacuation site(s).

5. Use walkie/talkies, cell phones, bullhorns and adult runners to communicate and confirm that the school has been cleared.

6. Designated staff members should account for all students by checking with teachers in the evacuation site(s).

7. Designated staff members should survey students at the assembly point to check for injuries or trauma and alert staff members trained in CPR and First Aid.

8. Call 911 or emergency services if there are injuries.

9. Contact School district service center to inspect school for possible damage.

10. No one should reenter the school until it has been determined to be safe by emergency management agency or building inspector.

11. Call school district office.

12. If the seismic activity damaged the school, the decision to open or close the school the next school day and subsequent days should be made jointly by the following only after a school building inspector has determined that the school structure is safe to reenter.

   - ✓ Superintendent's office
   - ✓ Principal and staff members
   - ✓ Law enforcement
   - ✓ Local County Emergency Personnel

13. Administrative staff members, with assistance from the School System Information Office and/or the Crisis Management Team, should prepare a written statement to be sent home with students.

14. The school district office should inform the local news media to announce the decision to open or close the school to the public.

Utility Emergency Protocol

(Electrical power failure, natural gas line break or leak, water main or sewer

break)

Most local fire departments and public safety departments will not allow students to remain in a school if the water to the school has been cut-off or compromised, due to safety of the water and lack of water pressure for fire suppression. Also, most local fire departments and public safety departments will not allow students to remain in a school for more than one or two hours after a power failure, due to hazardous conditions and a compromised fire alarm system. Consequently, schools may be forced to dismiss early. However, if the power fails and the school does not have a generator or backup battery powered fire alarm system, the school's Crisis Management Team should be alerted and placed with bullhorns throughout the school in case an emergency occurs during the power failure, which would allow for emergency communications.

Natural gas line break or leak

1. If during school hours, the school should be evacuated immediately.

2. Alert the school's Crisis Management Team.

3. Staff members and students move to the predetermined assembly points 1,000 feet away from the school using predetermined routes and exits.

4. Ensure that all staff members and students have left the school. Check hallways, restrooms, lounges, cafeterias, auditoriums, and gymnasiums.

5. Designated staff members should take the Crisis Emergency Kit to the evacuation site (s).

6. Use walkie/talkies, cell phones, bullhorns and adult runners to communicate and confirm that the school has been cleared.

7. Designated staff members should account for all students by checking with teachers in the evacuation site(s).

8. Designated staff members should survey students at the assembly point to check for injuries or trauma.

9. Call 911 or emergency services if there are injuries.

10. Everyone should remain in evacuation sites until the "all clear" signal/message is given.   Once students are in the school, use intercom to explain situation.

11. Contact School district service center to inspect school for possible damage or danger.

12. Call school district office.

13. Administrative staff members, with assistance from the School System Information Office and/or the Crisis Management Team, should prepare a written statement to be sent home with students.

Bacteria or Microorganism Threat Protocol

This includes receipt of or threat to receive a bacteria-laced or microorganism-laced letter, box, container, or envelope.

Preparedness

Staff members who handle mail and packages at the school should be alert to unusual packages, letters, or conditions, such as:

1. Excess postage on a small package or letter

2. No postage or non-canceled postage

3. Handwritten notes such as "to be opened by Mr. Smith"

4. Leaks, stains, sharp points or powdery substances on or in the package or letter

5. Anything that looks or feels like a wire or device inside the package or letter

Note: Students and volunteers should NOT be allowed to open or handle school mail.

Response to a Suspicious Package

1. Call 911 where available or call emergency services.

2. Alert the school's Crisis Management Team.

3. Isolate letter or package.

4. Evacuate and seal off the area of school.

5. Assign staff members to prevent others from entering the area.

6. Isolate staff members who may have contact with letter or package. Do not allow anyone else to touch it and take the staff members who touched the item to the school nurse.

7. Identify victims fully with name, address, and telephone number for first responders and health officials.

8. Assign staff members to make certain the school parking lot area is clear so first responders can reach the school with equipment.

9. Assign staff members to stand outside of the school to receive first responders in order to direct them to the student or staff member.

10. Based on the advice and instructions of first responders, be prepared to evacuate the school using standard evacuation procedures.

    ✓ Staff members and students move to the predetermined assembly points 1,000 feet away from the school using predetermined routes and exits (**NOTE**: administrators must re-direct classes if the predetermined routes pass near the hostage/barricade area.)

    ✓ Ensure that all staff members and students have left the school. Check hallways, restrooms, lounges, cafeterias, auditoriums, and gymnasiums.

    ✓ Designated staff members should take the Crisis Emergency Kit to the evacuation site (s).

    ✓ Use walkie/talkies, cell phones, bullhorns and adult runners to communicate and confirm that the school has been cleared.

    ✓ Designated staff members should account for all students by checking with teachers in the evacuation site (s).

    ✓ Designated staff members should survey students at the assembly point to check for injuries or trauma.

    ✓   Everyone should remain in evacuation sites until the "all clear" signal/message is given. Once students are in the school, use intercom to explain situation.

11. Emergency first responders will assess the package or letter to determine the potential danger.

12. School district office should determine when the school is ready to resume normal operations and announce to the news media and parents.

13. Administrative staff members, with assistance from the School System Information Office, should prepare a written statement to be sent home with students.

Additional Information about Responding to a Crisis

Information needed by first responders, 911 operators, and district office staff members:

1. Name of person calling

2. School name

3. Description of the incident

4. Names of people involved

5. Grade of students involved

6. Injuries (if applicable)

7. Damage (if applicable)

8. What action the school has taken thus far

9. Other information that impacts the school

10. Provide phone numbers to school, including private numbers and cell phone numbers

11. If incident necessitates someone coming to the school, give specific instructions (e.g., where to park, who to meet, what door to use, etc.) and always have a staff member available to meet the first responders.

How to Respond to the News Media

1. Greet the reporter/crew politely. Direct them to a predesignated area at the school, on the school campus or at the evacuation site.

2. Call the school district office. Request that someone come to the scene as the official spokesperson.

3. Tell the reporter/crew that students may not be interviewed or photographed during a crisis or at other time without parent permission.

Create a List of Quick Reference Phone Numbers

1. Superintendent's Office

2. School district office

3. Crisis Management Team (or Support Services)

4. Local utility provider hotline phone numbers

5. Local government departments, including water and sewer, parks and recreation, law enforcement, code enforcement, roads and bridges, transportation, etc.

6. School district maintenance staff members

7. School district transportation

8. Poison Control Emergency Phone Number

Chapter Nine

Crisis Preparedness and Response Protocols for Other Settings and

Situations

The secret of getting ahead is getting started.

-Mark Twain

There are locations and circumstances that require a different set of crisis procedures that are unique to potential and actual crises. These should be included in Crisis Management Plans, as well as any other situations, locations and circumstances that are unique to a school.

Stadium Emergency Evacuation Protocol

1. In stadiums the primary route of evacuation is to the playing field and then to outlying areas adjacent to the field, unless otherwise directed by law enforcement officers. This prevents bottlenecks at exits that could create a dangerous situation causing injuries. Also, the parents of students on the playing field may try to go to the field area at the same time others are moving to the exits. If everyone is moving in the same direction, it is more orderly and safer.

    Note: school districts need to assess their stadiums to make certain that there are sufficient exits from the bleachers/stadium seats onto the playing field to accommodate large crowds.

2. In the event of an emergency, all persons should move to the exits leading to the playing field in an orderly fashion, unless otherwise directed by law enforcement officers. This prevents bottlenecks at exits that could create a dangerous situation causing injuries. Also, the parents of students on the playing field may try to go to the field area at the same time others are moving to the exits. If everyone is moving in the same direction, it is more orderly and safer.

3. Persons should not exit to the parking lot, unless directed to do so by law enforcement officers.

4. Once on the playing field, all persons should move to the exits, as directed by law enforcement officers.

5. For persons in the concession area during a crisis evacuation, they should move to the closest exit, as directed by law enforcement officers.

Note: The family and friend reunification point after the crisis situation has ended is the playing field. At that time, law enforcement personnel will determine and announce when persons may return to the parking lots.

Other Possible Hazards

Is the school near an airport?

If "yes," does the school have an evacuation plan based on the location of the airport and flight patterns? Does the airport staff member know how to communicate with the school in the event of an emergency at or near the airport? Does the school have a method to communicate with the airport staff members? Does the local fire department have an airport emergency plan; if so, does it include the school?

Is the school near above-ground chemical storage tanks or an industrial park?

If "yes," does the school have an evacuation plan based on the location of the storage tanks or industrial park? Does the chemical storage company or companies in the industrial park know how to communicate with the school in the event of an emergency? Does the school have a method to communicate with companies with the chemical storage tanks or with companies in the industrial park? Does the school have identified staff members that can turn off the HVAC fresh-air mix? Does the local fire department have an emergency plan? If so, does it include the school?

Is the school near railroad tracks?

If "yes," does the school have an evacuation plan based on a possible derailment? Does the local fire department have an emergency plan? If so, does it include the school?

Chapter Ten

Pandemic Planning

Without such a solid, strategic alignment between the goals, people, and resources, crisis leadership interventions are at best futile and at worst disastrous.

-Bill Sedlacek

Most school district Crisis Management Plans do not include a section for pandemics or epidemics, even though the World Health Organization and CDC predict that pandemics such as the one in 2009 with the H1N1 influenza virus may be a prelude to future infections of that type.

A distinction should be made between an epidemic and a pandemic. An epidemic is a disease that temporarily is prevalent in a community or throughout a large area. A pandemic is a global outbreak.

Detailed information and suggestions for local plan development is provided in this chapter. It should be noted that while these guidelines focus on a pandemic, many of the prevention and operational plans could be applied to an epidemic event.

During times of crisis, schools rely heavily on the assistance of local community responders and agencies, particularly local boards of health. Relationships with these groups need to be established and cultivated long before a crisis occurs. Working with local agencies before a pandemic will decrease fear, anxiety and confusion and improve the response during a crisis. It is imperative for all school districts to collaborate with their local emergency management coordinators, their local public health officials, and other community stakeholders to create a crisis pandemic plan to assure a comprehensive and effective response.

This chapter includes specific considerations and examples to consider when developing a pandemic plan: prevention and education; access control; surveillance and screening; infection control and precautions; communication methods for staff members, parents, and community; school activities and operations; local and state responsibilities; recovery and resources.

Background and History of Pandemics

The first recorded influenza pandemic was in 1510, when an influenza virus spread throughout Africa and Europe. Epidemiological historians believe other influenza pandemics occurred between the 16th century and the 19th century, but the details are unclear.

The Asiatic Flu was first reported in May of 1889 in Russia. It spread rapidly west and reached North America in December of 1889. In 1890, it spread to South America, India, and Australia. This influenza pandemic was caused by the H2N8 type of flu virus and had a very high attack and mortality rate.

The Spanish Flu lasted from 1918-1919. It was first identified in March of 1918 in United States military personnel at Camp Funston, Kansas. By October of 1918, it had spread to become a worldwide pandemic. In just six months, 25 million people died worldwide. An estimated 500,000 died in the United States.

From 1957-1958, the Asian flu caused an estimated 70,000 deaths in the United States and 1.5 million worldwide. First identified in China in late February, 1957, the virus had spread to the United States by June. It lasted well into 1958.

The Hong Kong Flu, 1968-1969, was an Influenza A virus that caused about 35,000 deaths in the United States and 700,000 worldwide. The virus was first detected in Hong Kong in January of 1968 and reached the United States by June. Deaths from the virus continued into 1969.

Influenza, commonly called "the flu," is caused by the influenza virus, which infects the respiratory tract (nose, throat, lungs). Influenza usually spreads from person to person when an infected person coughs, sneezes, or talks, and the virus is sent into the air. Influenza can cause illness in all ages, and it is more likely than other viral respiratory infections, such as the common cold, to cause severe illness and life-threatening complications. Annually, more than 200,000 people in the United States are hospitalized from influenza. Approximately 36,000 people die from the flu and its complications every year. Should an influenza pandemic occur, the incidence of illness and death from influenza will likely dramatically increase worldwide.

The 2009 H1N1 (Swine Flu) outbreak is an example of how quickly a flu virus can spread between and among people.

Unique Features of Pandemics

Public Health authorities have identified characteristics and challenges unique to a pandemic such as:

1. When the pandemic influenza virus emerges, its global spread is considered inevitable.

2. Most people will have little or no immunity to a pandemic flu virus, and a significant percentage of the population could require medical care.

3. Death rates could be unpredictable due to the significant number of people who become infected, the virulence of the virus, and the characteristics and vulnerability of affected populations (elderly, those with chronic disease, and children).

4. Past pandemics have spread globally in two, and sometimes three, waves.

5. Medical supplies may be inadequate. Vaccine for the virus may not be available for months.

6. Hospital beds and other supplies may be limited.

7. Pandemics may also cause economic and social disruption such as schools and businesses closing, travel bans, and canceling of community events.

8. Care of sick family members and fear of exposure can result in significant absenteeism in the workforce.

At present, a primary concern is with the Avian Flu (H5N1), also called the Bird Flu, because the mortality rate is exceedingly high. The Avian Flu is an outbreak of a type of flu virus that may spread rapidly from one country to another. This virus affects only birds or animals at first. Health officials have confirmed this novel virus subtype and the fact that humans do not have immunities to it. Additionally, there are cases where humans have become infected with the virus and have become severely ill. The Avian Flu has not yet developed to the stage where the virus is easily transferred from human to human, but that may change in the future.

A cross-virus that could develop from a virus such as Swine Flu (H1N1) comingling with another type of virus could spread more quickly than the Avian Flu because it transfers from human to human easily, just as easily as seasonal flu. This type of virus may not have a high mortality rate, but the outbreak spread could quickly infect large numbers of citizens. If this type of flu evolves, the rapidity of the event may dictate a quick response from school districts to implement social distancing and other measures.

Symptoms of flu viruses in humans have ranged from typical influenza-like symptoms, such as fever, cough, sore throat, muscle aches and eye infections to more serious conditions such as pneumonia, acute respiratory distress, viral pneumonia, and other severe and life-threatening complications. Pre-existing physical conditions such as asthma may result in serious illness from a pandemic flu virus.

Impact of Pandemics on States

The United States Department of Health and Human Services (HHS) has provided a state-by-state estimate of the possible impact of a pandemic. The estimates are divided into two categories: A Moderate 1958 or 1968-like Outbreak and a Severe 1918-like Outbreak. To illustrate the possible impact at the state level, consider a state with a population of ten million people. In a Moderate Outbreak scenario, approximately 2.2 million people would become ill. Over 450,000 would require outpatient treatment and over 24,500 would need hospitalization. An estimated 6,100 would die from a Moderate Outbreak impact virus. In a Severe Outbreak scenario, approximately 2.2 million would become ill and over 450,000 citizens would require outpatient treatment. However, almost 60,000 would need hospital treatment and over 14,000 deaths would occur from a Severe Outbreak impact virus.

Even with a Moderate Outbreak, health care systems would be strained, as would other essential services. There may be business and school closures during a Moderate Outbreak. A Severe Outbreak would most likely require widespread, if not complete, school closures and would impact almost every segment of society.

It should be noted that the 1918 flu outbreak impacted almost every town, city and community in most states, even the most remote small towns and communities. With modern transportation capability and mobility of citizens, a present day outbreak could spread more completely and rapidly than the 1918 outbreak.

Pandemic Crisis Planning

A school district's pandemic plan would also be relevant and essential in the event of a localized or regional epidemic. The plan would also be critically important if widespread vaccinations were necessary.

Points to Consider During Planning for a Pandemic

In planning for a pandemic or epidemic event, schools and school districts should consider the following:

School Impact and Issues

1. Potential for school closings: full school closure or partial school closure where some schools are closed while others remain open

2. Large numbers of staff members absent, difficult to maintain school operations

3. Loss of services from suppliers (e.g. food services and transportation)

4. Student absenteeism elevated above normal trends

5. Parents who choose to keep healthy children at home

Community Considerations

1. Large percentages of the population may be unable to work for days to weeks during a pandemic.

2. Significant numbers of people and expertise would be unavailable.

3. Emergency and essential services such as fire, police, and medical could be diminished.

4. School operations could be affected.

5. Methods of continued instruction should schools close

Basic Goals in Pandemic Planning

1. Limit illness, the spread of illness, and emotional trauma

2. Preserve continuity of essential functions

3. Minimize social and educational disruption

4. Minimize instructional loss

Key Components to Pandemic Planning

1. Education and Prevention

   ✓ Educating school district staff members, students, and parents about good hygiene practices is a significantly important component of illness prevention and control.

2. Incident Command System

   ✓ Establishing an Incident Command System will be essential for managing any type of emergency or event like a pandemic

3. Communication

   ✓ Establishing communication protocols and links is essential now, before an emergency like a pandemic emerges.

   ✓ The communication protocol should include internal and external emergency contact lists and methods.

   ✓ The communication lists should be updated and verified on a regular basis.

4. Stakeholder Coordination

    ✓ The school district's pandemic planning team should work with local public health officials.

5. Surveillance (student and staff attendance)

    ✓ The school district and the local health department should work together to establish a "sentinel" program to monitor student and staff members attendance. For example, when student attendance drops below 90 percent, the school district sends a notice to the local health department. Student and staff member absences may be an early indicator of a widespread virus event.

6. Prepare for Partial or Full Closing of Schools or School District

    ✓ School and staff members assignments

    ✓ Bus routes

    ✓ Work on plans with local agencies to assist families

7. Alternatives to Closing Schools

    ✓ Implement social distancing.

    ✓ Eliminate field trips.

    ✓ Reduce or postpone extracurricular activities.

    ✓ Set "screeners" at school entrance to screen out students and staff members with flu-like symptoms to prevent them from going to classes.

8. Educational Continuity

    ✓ In the event that schools or school districts have to close, what strategies will be in place to continue education in some form? How will school work continue for students whose school is closed while other schools remain open in the same school district? This difficult task should be part of the pandemic planning team's discussions and plans.

9. Recovery

   ✓ Each school district's pandemic plan should address the complexities of recovery. This document provides an example of Recovery Phases, including recovery of essential services and health concerns prior to reopening schools.

Pandemic Planning Team Responsibilities and Considerations

1. Develop the preparedness and pandemic response plan using levels, as suggested in this manual; include Decision Forms to create a decision archive for the event.

2. Identify school authorities responsible for activating the pandemic influenza plan.

3. Consider and provide sufficient and accessible infection prevention supplies.

4. Consider provision of sufficient school operation supplies (food, cleaning supplies, paper supplies) during a pandemic when schools are open.

5. Develop a process with the local public health director to report a substantial increase in absenteeism among students and faculty.

6. Identify methods to reduce the spread of the virus.

7. Plan for the identification and screening of students and staff members with flu-like symptoms.

8. Plan for the care of students who are ill and determine when ill students may return to school. Determine how ill students at school will be isolated until parents arrive.

9. Plan for continuity of operations and identify essential services.

10. Communicate the plan to division administrative staff members, school staff members, parents/guardians, students, and the community.

11. Provide information to families for development of individual family plans.

12. Plan for the delivery of educational services in the event that a significant number of staff members become ill.

13. Plan for the orderly closure or partial closure of school operations, ongoing instruction, and eventual school reopening.

14. Coordinate school closure or partial closure with neighboring school districts.

15. Discuss the needs of international students, disabled students, and impoverished students.

16. Plan for the use of school facilities by community partners during a pandemic if the schools are closed or partially closed (i.e., vaccinations).

17. Test the plan; conduct table-top exercises (include local health department).

Pandemic Response Recommendations and Planning Components

Information regarding the occurrence of a pandemic in a community is typically provided by the state and local health departments and others designated at the state level. States' response to a pandemic should be guided by the World Health Organization (WHO), United States Department of Health and Human Services, CDC, and the recommendations of a state's division of public health.

This section of the chapter includes pandemic operational actions "Levels" that are paired with the United States Government's pandemic "Stages" system, which are both overlaid by the World Health Organization's pandemic "Phases." The Levels serve as an example to school districts to guide development of responses and actions based on the identification and evolution of a pandemic event. This system of levels, stages and phases should help school districts specify timely operational responses and decisions. This section of the chapter also includes a Decision-Making Matrix that helps delineate areas of decision responsibilities during a pandemic event, so school districts can focus on local operational planning. It should be noted that the decision whether or not to close schools rests with the local boards of education, based on public health information and guidance.

The levels include specific considerations during each event level of the pandemic and are matched with United States Government (USG) Stages. Local school districts, based on their local pandemic plan, can take action at each event level. The following provides suggestions and examples for activities and operational plans in response to the spread of a pandemic. It is not intended to cover or include all activities or strategies. It should be noted that, depending on circumstances, it is possible a pandemic would spread rapidly within a few days, so schools may have to close at some time during Levels 3-6. It is also possible that some schools will close while others remain open, depending on circumstances such as the spread of the virus and the intensity of the virus.

(NOTE: Depending on circumstances, it may be necessary to either move rapidly from one level to another or even skip levels in order to respond to event circumstances.)

Level 0: Prevention and Preparations

1. Place posters on hand washing and infection control in schools and on website.

2. Provide information to schools, parents, and staff members about hand sanitizers, cough and sneeze etiquette, signs and symptoms of influenza.

3. Ensure custodial staff members have appropriate training on proper cleaning and disinfecting work and play areas.

4. Ensure schools and departments have adequate supplies (soaps, hand sanitizers, etc.).

5. Check First Aid Kits and add N95 face masks for school nurses and other staff members.

6. Establish and test emergency communication protocol with staff members contact "tree."

7. Provide information to staff members and parents on pandemic planning for families.

8. Develop Incident Command Center protocol, location, equipment and assign staff members.

9. Develop plans for operating with staff members workforce reduction.

10. Develop plans to secure schools, information technology, and finance.

11. Encourage employees to use direct deposit for paychecks.

12. Encourage parents to have alternative child care plans.

13. Develop alternatives to closing schools (i.e., implement social distancing; eliminate field trips; reduce or postpone extracurricular activities; set "screeners" at school entrance to screen out students and staff members with flu-like symptoms to prevent them from going to classes.)

14. Develop plans for educational continuity if schools close:

    a. Study packets and suggested activities for students and parents

    b. Web-based education (i.e., on-line classes; virtual school; education blogs; home school educational websites)

15. Find out if vendors in the supply chain have a pandemic or emergency plan for continuity or recovery of supply deliveries.

16. Plan for full school district closure and partial school closure (i.e., some schools closed while others remain open within the same school district).

17. Develop a mental health plan for students and staff members, in conjunction with local mental health services staff members to implement during a pandemic event and during the recovery phase; the plan should include post-traumatic stress syndrome counseling.

18. Develop Human Resources employee emergency contact lists and reciprocal contact procedures; Human Resources should conduct a study of critical infrastructure staff members with young children (because they are more likely to remain home during a widespread illness event) to determine if redundancy plans are necessary; develop a Fitness for Duty checklist to determine if an employee is ready to return to work and under what conditions.

19. Local school superintendent should establish a command structure in the event that he or she is unable to continue work during the pandemic event or is unable to return to work during the recovery

phase; develop school district office teleconferencing protocol in the event that schools are closed.

20. Develop plans to conduct table-top exercises to practice and refine pandemic plan.

21. Apply all plans and procedures to after-school programs.

Level 1: Suspected Human-to-Human Outbreak

1. Review pandemic plan for preparedness and provide ongoing communication to key staff members on their roles and responsibilities.

2. Maintain infection control precautionary measures.

3. Keep staff members and parents current with updates through the school district website and cable access channel, if available; ask PTA or PTSA to assist with updated messages; make certain that health-related information and pandemic updates have been verified for accuracy by the local health department.

4. Ensure all staff members and external contact information is current, including direct lines to the local health department.

5. Open direct link to local health department.

6. Alert all principals of Event Level 1 status and remind them that the Event Level may escalate rapidly to the next Level or Levels.

7. Monitor student and staff member attendance daily and report to the local health department any school where student and/or staff members attendance drops below 90 percent.

8. Review out-of-country field trips and plans for future out-of-country field trips. Cancel out-of-country field trips to countries with human-to-human outbreak; review out-of-state field trips and inform schools and parents that all future field trips may be cancelled.

9. Do not enroll students from out-of-country or out-of-state without appropriate immunization records, based on immunization and other health guidelines provided by the local health department, the state department of public health and/or the United States Department of Health and Human Services.

10. Place Incident Command Center staff members on standby; remind appropriate staff members of Incident Command Center duties and responsibilities.

11. Provide information to the local health department on medically fragile children that may need specialized care at school or at home during a pandemic event; share local health department contact information with the parents of medically fragile children and provide guidance on how and who to contact at the local health department if their medically fragile child or children are at home due to long-term public and school closure.

12. Inform community agencies and non-profit agencies (i.e., Public health, Red Cross, Traveler's Aid, etc.) of families that may not have access to food on a regular basis, that may have a language barrier that would impede their efforts to seek basic essentials during an outbreak, or other families that would have limited resources during a long-term outbreak.

13. Meet with all daycare providers that use school district facilities or who receive students after school via school district school buses to inform them of pandemic response procedures and keep them up-to-date on health information and operational procedures.

14. Apply all procedures to after-school programs.

Level 2: Confirmed Human Outbreak

1. Conduct meeting with Incident Command Center staff members to pre-stage full activation of Center.

2. Provide ongoing communication to key staff members on their roles and responsibilities.

3. Maintain infection control precautionary measures.

4. Keep staff members and parents current with updates through the school district website and cable access channel, if available; ask PTA or PTSA to assist with updated messages; make certain that health-related information and pandemic updates have been verified for accuracy by the local health department.

5. Alert all principals of Event Level 2 status and remind them that the Event Level may escalate rapidly to the next Level or Levels.

6. Monitor student and staff member attendance daily and report to the local health department any school where student and/or staff members attendance drops below 90 percent.

7. Do not enroll any students without appropriate immunization records, based on immunization and other health guidelines provided by the local health department, the state department of public health and/or the United States Department of Health and Human Services.

8. Develop continuous direct link to local health department; make plans with the local health department to establish daily communications if a widespread outbreak occurs overseas.

9. Continue surveillance of staff members, students, school visitors, and other personnel to help the local health department to monitor influenza-like symptoms; it would be helpful to local health departments if these reports at this level could be provided on a daily basis.

10. Activate procedures to isolate students and staff members that present flu-like symptoms; encourage parents to keep their children

at home if they have flu-like symptoms and to let the school know about their child's symptoms; encourage staff members to remain at home if they have flu-like symptoms and to report these symptoms to the school.

11. Keep relevant groups informed through cable access channel, e-mails, newsletters, fact sheets, and websites (i.e., booster clubs, activity clubs).

12. Meet with hot-line information staff members to review possible activation of the hot-line information based on events occurring at this time.

13. Remind staff members, students, and parents of good hygiene practices.

14. Consider cancelling all out-of-country field trips or alert the chaperones.

15. Review all out-of-state (in-country) field trips and be prepared to cancel all out-of-state field trips. Alert parents that future field trips may be cancelled.

16. Do not allow students or staff members into school who are presenting influenza-like symptoms; monitor students and staff members closely for flu-like symptoms.

17. Prepare to implement educational continuity plans.

18. Apply all procedures to after-school programs.

Level 3: Widespread Human Outbreak

1. Activation of Incident Command Center and pre-stage 24/7 manning of Center; bring in extra phones (and cell phones) and computers; meet with Incident Command Center staff members to prepare for rapid escalation of outbreak to North America; remind staff members of roles and responsibilities and importance of access at any time.

2. Activate daily direct link to local health department and, if possible, to the State Emergency Operations Center and/or the state department of public health.

3. Pre-stage information hotline for parents and staff members; alert information hotline staff members to report for a practice run of the hotline.

4. Keep staff members and parents current with updates through the school district website and cable access channel, if available; ask PTA or PTSA to assist with updated messages; make certain that health-related information and pandemic updates have been verified for accuracy by the local health department.

5. Alert all principals of Event Level 3 status and remind them that the Event Level may escalate rapidly to the next Level or Levels.

6. Monitor student and staff member attendance daily and report to the local health department.

7. Alert school district office staff members to possible full school district or partial school closure.

8. Alert school district office staff members to possible cancellation of extracurricular activities.

9. Continue surveillance of staff members, students, school visitors, and other personnel to help the local health department to monitor influenza-like symptoms; it would be helpful to local health departments if these reports at this level could be provided on a daily basis.

10. Cancel and call back all out-of-state field trips and ensure that all out-of-country field trips have been cancelled and called back.

11. Do not enroll new students without immunization records or approval from the local health department, based on immunization and other health guidelines provided by the local health department, the state department of public health and/or the United States Department of Health and Human Services.

12. Sanitize schools and buses daily, as per local health department guidelines; implement sanitizing verification process.

13. Restrict school visitors to parents and vendors; be alert to parents or vendors with flu-like symptoms.

14. Isolate ill students and staff members in pre-determined locations in the school with supervision until they can be sent home or picked up by authorized persons.

15. Pre-stage Crisis Management Team to discuss updated pandemic information and possible timeline for activation of the Team (or teams.)

16. Pre-stage educational continuity plans.

17. Apply all procedures to after-school programs; provide daily updated outbreak information to after-school programs and staff members.

Level 4: Expanded Human Outbreak

1. Full activation of Incident Command Center for all direct report staff members, with direct link to local health department and, if possible, to the State Emergency Operations Center and/or the state department of public health.

2. Alert Secondary Incident Command Center staff members, in case primary staff members are unable to man the Incident Command Center.

3. Activate information hotline for parents and staff members; update hotline information daily (at least), website information, and provide media updates (in collaboration with local health department and/or the state department of public health); make certain that health-related information and pandemic updates have been verified for accuracy by the local health department and/or the state department of public health.

4. Activate Crisis Management Team for student and staff member psychological support.

5. Closely monitor staff members and student attendance and provide reports to the local health department twice daily and to the Incident Command Center.

6. Do not enroll new students without immunization records or approval from the local health department, based on immunization and other health guidelines provided by the local health department, the state department of public health and/or the United States Department of Health and Human Services.

7. Human Resources reports to the Incident Command Center when any school, service, or support absences escalate.

8. Human Resources contacts substitute teachers to determine availability.

9. Pre-stage implementation of Educational Continuity Plans (i.e., study packets; cable access; local library system; on-line classes, etc.).

10. Pre-stage alternatives to school closure:

    a. Gatherings of groups larger than normal class size may be limited during the school day (e.g. assemblies, recess).

    b. Prepare for possible cancellation of extracurricular activities.

    c. All field trips cancelled or called back.

    d. Review extracurricular activities.

    e. Do not accept students or staff members with flu-like symptoms.

    f. Student distance spacing strategies to decrease contact with students who may be infected, but are not exhibiting symptoms.

        i. It is recommended that students' desks be spaced three (3) feet apart.
        ii. Discourage prolonged congregation in hall ways and lunchrooms.
        iii. Limit group activities and interaction between classes.
        iv. Cancel or modify gym class, choir or other school activities that place individuals in close proximity.

11. Pre-stage partial school closure or full school closure.

12. Isolate and send home staff members or students with flu-like symptoms.

13. An appropriate room for isolation should have been designated and will be utilized and supervised at this time. Access to this room should be strictly limited and monitored.

14. A school bus may be designated to transport sick students home (buses should be used in this capacity ONLY as an emergency measure when no one is available to pick the child up at school); buses should have an adult monitor.

15. Students and staff members with flu-like symptoms will be asked to stay home. Absences should be reported to the school attendance office throughout the school day, instead of once a day.

16. Those allowed into the school will be screened for flu-like symptoms. Each person cleared to enter the school will be given something to indicate that they are free to enter the school (e.g. a sticker, a card, a stamp on their hand).

17. Adults and students accompanied by an adult may be excluded from entry into the school and instructed to call their health care providers for advice and evaluation.

18. If a person warrants medical evaluation, health services staff members should alert the local health department that a suspect case needs evaluation so that the health department can provide guidance.

19. Alter school cleaning routines by maintenance staff members.

    a. Disinfect work areas, counters, restrooms, door knobs, and stair railings more frequently.

    b. The school health office and holding areas for ill children should be cleaned at least twice each day and preferably throughout the day, in the morning before students arrive and in the afternoon after students leave the area.

    c. Air conditioning system filters should be cleaned and changed frequently.

    d. Telephones, pencils, pens, etc. should not be shared.

    e. Specialized cleaning solutions are not essential. Standard cleaning products can disinfect surfaces (note: soap and water may not disinfect surfaces). The frequency of cleaning is most important.

    f. During the day, where operationally possible, increase ventilation to the facility to decrease spread of disease. Following each school day, the   school should be thoroughly ventilated and cleaned: opening all doors and windows or turning the air conditioning/heating systems up.

20. Apply all procedures to after-school programs; provide daily updated outbreak information to after-school programs and staff members.

Level 5: Expanded (local) Outbreak

1. Full activation of Incident Command Center 24/7

2. Maintain daily link to local health department and, if possible, to the State Emergency Operations Center and/or the state department of public health.

3. Prepare for communication links from public health and state department of education

4. Human Resources reports to the Incident Command Center when any school, service, or support absences escalate.

5. Partial school or full school closure or alternatives to closure, as recommended by public health.

6. All field trips cancelled or called back, including local field trips.

7. Cancellation of extracurricular activities.

8. Prepare Educational Continuity Plans (i.e., study packets; cable access; local library system; on-line classes, etc.) for rapid activation.

    a. Pre-developed Study Packets and suggested activities for students

    b. Web-based education:

        i. On-line classes

        ii. Virtual school

        iii. Education Blogs

        iv. Home school educational websites

9. Do not enroll new students without immunization records or approval from the local health department, based on immunization and other health guidelines provided by the local health department, the Georgia Division of Public Health and/or the United States Department of Health and Human Services.

10. Expand hotline staff members and update hotline information, website information, and provide media updates; provide updates from public health department, from the district superintendent, and, if necessary, from local law enforcement and public utilities and services; encourage parents to keep ill children at home and encourage ill staff members to remain at home.

11. Monitor students getting off buses and out of vehicles for signs of flu-like symptoms; do not accept students or staff members with flu-like symptoms, **or** quickly isolate students and staff members with flu-like symptoms.

12. Isolate and send home staff members or students with flu-like symptoms, utilizing supervised isolation areas in the school; access to this room should be strictly limited and monitored (i.e., parents picking up their ill children should be escorted to and from the isolation area); a carefully monitored student checkout system should be activated.

13. A school bus may be designated to transport sick students home; the school bus or buses should include adult monitors who may be asked to walk students to their homes from the bus (buses should be used in this capacity ONLY as an emergency measure when no one is available to pick the child up at school).

14. Students and staff members who have flu-like symptoms should be asked to stay home; add this information to the information hot-line.

15. Absences should be reported to the school attendance office throughout the day, and staff members' absences reported to Human Resources as soon as possible, but at least twice daily.

16. Access to the school will be limited; persons presenting flu-like symptoms will not be allowed into the school; if a parent is at school to pick up his or her child before normal dismissal, the student will be brought to the parent outside the school; each person cleared to enter the school will be given something to indicate that they are free to enter the school (e.g. a sticker, a card, a stamp on their hand).

17. If a person warrants medical evaluation, health services staff members should alert the appropriate medical resources (i.e., public health) that a suspect case needs evaluation so that the referral center can make arrangements for a health assessment.

18. Activate social distancing strategies:

    a. Gatherings of groups larger than normal class size should be cancelled and avoided (e.g. assemblies, recess).

    b. Cancel all extra-curricular activities.
    c. Student distance spacing strategies to decrease contact with students who may be infected but not exhibiting symptoms.

        i. Separate student desks as much as possible

        ii. Prohibit congregation in hall ways and lunchrooms; if possible, serve box lunches in classrooms to avoid gathering of students in the cafeteria; stagger class changes to avoid large groups of students in the hallway; stagger dismissal for the same reason; cancel gym class, choir or other school activities that place individuals in close proximity.

        iii. If possible stagger bus routes to reduce the number of students on each bus.

19. Expand school cleaning routines by maintenance staff members.

    a. Disinfect all work areas, counters, restrooms, door knobs, and stair railings several times daily; use other staff members to assist, if necessary (specialized cleaning solutions are not essential; standard cleaning products can disinfect surfaces; the frequency of cleaning is most important).

    b. The school health office and holding areas for ill children and staff members should be cleaned several times each day.

    c. Air conditioning system filters should be cleaned and changed frequently.

    d.   Telephones, pencils, pens, etc. should not be shared.

    e.   During the day, where operationally possible, increase ventilation to the facility to decrease spread of disease. Following each school day, the school should be thoroughly ventilated and cleaned: opening all doors and windows or turning the air conditioning/heating systems up.

20. Apply all procedures to after-school programs; provide daily updated outbreak information to after-school programs and staff members.

Level 6: Health Emergency

1. Based on a directive from public health, the Governor or a joint decision between public health and the local school system, the superintendent orders a partial closure of schools. Depending on circumstances, it may be one or more schools.

OR

2. Based on a directive from public health, the Governor or a joint decision between public health and the local school system, the superintendent closes all school school units and other department school units of the school district; the closure applies to all after-school programs and extracurricular activities. NOTE: It is possible that the first "order" or "recommendation" is to close only those schools with pandemic flu-related absences, so be prepared for partial school closures and preventing students from the affected school trying to enroll in other schools).

3. Confirm closure with the state department of education.

4. Inform the public and school district employees using all means of communication (i.e., press release; hotline recording; website emergency message; cable access; etc.); coordinate news release with public health and the state department of education.

5. Secure all schools.

6. School system police or other law enforcement agencies should check all schools and establish periodic patrols during the school closure period.

7. All perishable food items should be disposed of unless the cafeteria remains open.

8. Check all alarm and surveillance systems.

9. Secure information technology system and integrity.

10. Secure all school buses and service vehicles.

11. If possible, maintain Incident Command Center operations and essential services; if not possible, school district office staff members should maintain telephone contact on a regular basis with the superintendent, such as daily conference calls.

12. Maintain communications with the local health department through superintendent and/or designated staff members.

13. When possible, collaborate with local agencies to assist families.

14. Activate Educational Continuity Plan

    a. Distribute pre-developed study packets and suggested activities for students and parents

    b. Web-based education considerations:

        i. Cable Access educational television (with closed caption)

        ii. Cable Educational shows (with closed caption)

        iii. Video-streaming (with closed caption)

        iv. Textbook and study guide depositories with drive-through capabilities

        v. Virtual classes on-line

        vi. Teleconferencing

Levels 7: Recovery – Taking Steps to Reopen Schools

1. Based on communication with public health and authorization to start the process of recovery, the school district will begin the initial stages of preparations for the re-opening of schools.

2. Re-establish Incident Command Center as soon as possible.

3. Human Resources will begin the process of compiling phone tree results indicating which staff members are ready to return to work, **OR** establish an Employee Hotline Phone Bank so employees can call in status (name; position; work location; health status; return to work date); use a pre-determined Fitness for Duty checklist to determine if an employee is ready to return to work and under what conditions.

4. Human Resources will develop a status report for each staff member category by school and department: teachers, administrators, custodians, bus drivers, etc.

5. When possible, the Crisis Management Team staff members will meet to activate the mental health plan for students and staff members, in conjunction with local mental health services staff members, including Post-Traumatic Stress Syndrome counseling.

6. Inspect all schools, facilities, equipment, materials, etc. and determine status and needs for operations. Maintain a status update for facilities not ready for occupancy.

7. Inspect all buses.

8. Survey supply vendors to determine when supply chain and delivery system will be partially or fully operational; provide vendors with supply needs.

9. Finance department determines process for fast-tracking purchase orders for essential supplies.

10. Determine information technology status and operational needs; this will be related to financial technology, also.

11. Inspect all school cafeterias with the assistance of the local health department.

12. Expand school cleaning routines by maintenance staff members.

13. Disinfect all work areas, counters, restrooms, door knobs, and stair railings several times daily; use other staff members to assist, if necessary (specialized cleaning solutions are not essential; standard cleaning products can disinfect surfaces; the frequency of cleaning is most important).

14. Air conditioning system filters should be cleaned and changed.

15. The school should be thoroughly ventilated and cleaned: opening all doors and windows or turning the air conditioning/heating systems up.

16. Establish a timeline for opening schools and other schools for staff members, based on reports from Human Resources, school and bus inspections, and the local health department; determine which schools can open and if temporary consolidation of schools is appropriate. Include other agencies in the discussion about re-opening schools, such as DFCS, public health, mental health, Fire Marshal, law enforcement, public transportation, etc.

17. Share timeline for opening with news media and place recording on school district main phone line; also add to school district website.

18. Some schools may remain closed until facility and/or staffing requirements are met.

19. Re-activate information hot-line as soon as possible.

20. Post information on school district website for parents regarding helping children cope with tragedies (i.e., "Teaching Children How to Respond to Tragedies" from the National Association of School Psychologists).

21. Provide parents with an updated school year calendar.

22. Begin discussions on restructuring and resuming extra-curricular activities and after-school programs.

23. Opening of schools should be monitored closely by Command Center staff members.

24. Daily reports of staff members and student attendance should be closely monitored.

25. A mental health status report, based on guidelines provided by the counselors and the Crisis Management Team, should be provided to the Command Center each day. This report should include the mental status of students and staff members in order to determine if additional mental health services are needed.

26. School nurses should compile daily health reports for the Command Center.

27. Develop an "instructional reconstruction" checklist (base on the length of school closure; if short-term, the checklist should be focused on make-up work and reorganizing the instructional calendar, benchmarks, testing, etc.; if the closure was long-term, the checklist may require restructuring of the current and following school year instructional and operational calendar and events) to guide staff members, students, and parents when school reopens. The checklist should include anticipated instructional materials and supplies, as well as possible waivers from the state department of education.

28. Do not enroll new students without immunization records or approval from the local health department, based on immunization and other health guidelines provided by the local health department, state department of public health and/or the United States Department of Health and Human Services.

29. Even when schools re-open, many students may need homebound instruction. A possible shortage of homebound teachers may be mitigated by maintain the Educational Continuity Plan

    a. Distribute pre-developed study packets and suggested activities for students and parents

  b. Web-based education considerations:

    i. Cable Access educational television (with closed caption)

    ii. Cable Educational shows (with closed caption)

    iii. Video-streaming (with closed caption)

    iv. Textbook and study guide depositories with drive-through capabilities

    v. Teleconferencing

30. When schools re-open activate social distancing strategies (to minimize possible infection spread):

  a. Gatherings of groups larger than normal class size should be cancelled and avoided (e.g. assemblies, recess).

  b. Student distance spacing strategies to decrease contact with students who may be infected but not exhibiting symptoms.

    i. Separate student desks as much as possible

    ii. Prohibit congregation in hall ways and lunchrooms; if possible, serve box lunches in classrooms to avoid gathering of students in the cafeteria; stagger class changes to avoid large groups of students in the hallway; stagger dismissal for the same reason; cancel gym class, choir or other school activities that place individuals in close proximity.

    iii. If possible, stagger bus routes so there are fewer students on each bus.

Surveillance, Screening and Triage

During all stages of a pandemic flu outbreak, it will be essential to monitor and document the number of students and faculty who are absent and meet the definition of influenza-like illness. Keeping track of these numbers will help school and health officials determine when and whether to close schools, whether the epidemic is increasing in scope and whether to declare an epidemic, making schools eligible to apply for reimbursement of ADA funds during increased absenteeism.

1. School-level school health services personnel (registered nurses, licensed practical nurses, nursing assistants, or principal's designee) will develop a plan to screen all students and staff members. Younger children may be observed by health services personnel for cough. Older children may be asked the following question: "Do you have a new cough that has developed over the last 10 days?"

2. School health services personnel will provide staff members and students who have a new cough with tissues. Surgical masks are not appropriate for all situations, but are for specific health care situations.

3. School health services personnel will document screening data and review each week for analysis of trends.

4. The school nurse will evaluate individuals who have a new cough or fever (temperature ≥ 100.4) and place all individuals who have fever and a new cough on droplet precautions, pending further evaluation.

5. Students who have been identified as sick should be placed in an identified isolation room for sick children until picked up by parents.

6. Local school district health services staff members have the authority to restrict individuals (staff members and students) who have fever and a new cough from work, class, or any other group gathering. They also have the authority to send any student or staff member home. Absenteeism will be monitored for any trends. School health staff members will work with school administrators, social workers and attendance clerks to monitor absentee trends. Significant trends will be reported to the school nurse coordinator or school health

contract person, who will inform the Superintendent and the local health department.

7. Infection control posters will be placed at all school entrances and commons areas.

8. Poster information will include health tips for protection against the spread of the flu and other germs and viruses.

9. The school health services nurse coordinator will monitor national, regional, and local data related to epidemic respiratory infections.

Infection Control/Precautions

1. All staff members, students, and visitors will use droplet precautions (private room and surgical mask within 3 feet of ill person) for all contact with any individual who has a new cough and fever, until a diagnosis of a non-contagious respiratory illness, or an infection requiring a higher level of precautions is made.

2. If students, staff members or visitors present with symptoms while at school, they should be provided a mask while awaiting transportation away from the facility.

3. School staff members will ask persons who have a new cough to wear a surgical mask or use tissues to cover their mouth and nose when coughing, and to use proper hand hygiene during the time they need to be in the school (Note: wearing a surgical mask is not a guarantee of protection in a general setting).

4. Wash hands thoroughly and often: use soap and water and wash for at least 20 seconds. Use alcohol-based hand sanitizers when hand washing is not possible. It is advised that all classrooms have alcohol-based hand sanitizers available for use by students and staff members.

5. Schools will advise all persons, including staff members, students, and visitors, who have fever and cough to defer attending or visiting the school until their illness has resolved.

6. If an isolation room is in use, a precaution sign will be placed on the door.

7. Schools will maintain adequate supplies of surgical masks, waterless hand rub, surface cleaners and disinfectants, and tissues throughout public areas, classrooms, and meeting rooms and in the school health offices. All surfaces will be cleaned and disinfected with an Environmental Protection Agency (EPA)-registered household disinfectant labeled for activity against bacteria and viruses, an EPA-registered hospital disinfectant, or EPA-registered chlorine bleach/hypochlorite solution. Labeled instructions should always be followed when using any of these disinfectants.

8. Maintain appropriate inventories of supplies.

9. Protocols for waste disposal must be developed.

10. Schools will display hand-washing posters and "Cover Your Cough" posters in high-traffic areas and classrooms. Posters are available at *www.cde.gov/flu/protect/covercough*

Communication and Education

School districts will develop an effective and sustainable plan for communication and promotion of messages relating to epidemic respiratory infections to internal and external audiences.

1. Infection control measures will be reviewed with staff members, annually, as well as strategies for communicating information to health services providers in the event of an epidemic respiratory infection.

2. Translation services for languages in the represented student population will be provided.

3. A variety of media may be used to communicate with the school community including: newsletters, take-home flyers, messages on school menus, websites, school TV channels, county TV channels, and phone hotlines.

Additional Preparedness Activities

The following recommendations are for regular influenza season. Routine vaccination against seasonal influenza establishes good health practices and may boost the immune system during a pandemic flu outbreak. There will be a separate vaccination campaign that may take place during a pandemic.

1. School districts will encourage influenza vaccination during the influenza season to reduce morbidity from seasonal influenza transmission in school staff members.

2. All eligible staff members will be offered the opportunity to receive influenza vaccine. School districts can collaborate with local health departments for this service. School nurses in collaboration with local health departments can hold vaccination clinics on designated days.

3. School districts can provide staff members with information for local clinics providing the influenza vaccine.

4. Educational and promotional materials can be provided to school staff members to promote availability and desirability of influenza vaccine for all ages.

Regulatory Authority Regarding Public Health Matters

Regulatory authority is the power that the legislature gives an agency to enforce statutes, to develop regulations that have the force of law, and to assist the public in complying with laws and regulations. The power that can be delegated and the method of delegation are determined by the state or federal constitution. Some agencies are charged with enforcing specific statutes passed by a legislative body and given little discretion in their actions. Public health agencies are generally delegated broad authority and wide discretion to develop regulations and enforcement policies based on their expertise. When these regulations are published and adopted by the agency, they have the force of law unless they exceed the agency's statutory authority.

The most important regulatory authority delegated to public health agencies is the power to act quickly and flexibly—without promulgating formal regulations and without judicial hearings— when necessary to respond to exigent circumstances and to prevent abuse, hearings and other review proceedings after the action has been taken. More commonly, however, public health agencies promulgate specific regulations or adopt national codes as binding in their jurisdiction. These are enforced through licensing and other mechanisms that require regulated entities to adhere to the regulations. This provides clear guidance for the regulated entities and simplifies enforcement. Deviation from the standards is easily documented, preventing lengthy legal challenges to enforcement actions.

Roles of the Federal Government during a Pandemic

The federal government is responsible for nationwide coordination of the pandemic influenza response. Specific areas of responsibility include the following:

1. Surveillance in the U.S. and globally

2. Epidemiologic investigation in the U.S. and globally

3. Development and use of diagnostic laboratory tests and reagents

4. Development of reference strains for vaccines

5. Vaccine evaluation and licensure

6. Determination of populations at highest risk and strategies for vaccination/antiviral use

7. Assessment of measures to decrease transmission (e.g., travel restrictions, isolation, and quarantine)

8. Deployment of federally purchased vaccine

9. Deployment of antiviral agents that may be available as part of the Strategic National Stockpile

10. Evaluation of the efficacy of response measures

11. Evaluation of vaccine safety

12. Deployment of the Commissioned Corps Readiness Force (CCRF) and Epidemic Intelligence Service (EIS) officers

13. Medical and public health communications

14. Activation and deployment of additional regional, federal and Department of Defense resources

Typical Roles of State Division of Public Health Before and During a Pandemic

1. Establish a state pandemic planning executive committee.

2. Advocate the importance of pandemic planning to relevant decision-makers.

3. Periodically update plan in close collaboration with relevant partners, including those outside the health sector, and with reference to current WHO and CDC guidelines.

4. Ensure implementation of planning and preparedness activities at all levels of public authorities.

5. Exercise influenza pandemic plans and use the results to improve and refine plan and preparedness.

6. Identify crucial gaps in state and/or local infrastructure and resources, laws and/or statutes, which, if not corrected in advance, may interfere with an effective response.

7. Develop and maintain lists, including contact information, of partners, resources, and facilities.

8. Identify and brief regularly, as well as train key personnel to be mobilized in case of the emergence of a new strain of influenza virus.

9. Coordinate planning with bordering jurisdictions, including counties, states, and unique populations (such as new immigrant and refugee populations, and certain religious sectors).

10. Consider the development of a state stockpile (antivirals, personal protective equipment, vaccines, laboratory diagnostics, and other technical support) for rapid deployment when needed.

11. Ensure procedures for rapid sharing of specimens or isolates for virus characterization and development of diagnostics and vaccine.

12. Develop surge capacity contingency plans for the internal management of state resources and essential workers during a pandemic.

13. Influenza surveillance in several states includes 6 major components:

   ✓ Surveillance for influenza-like illness (ILI): Sentinel health-care providers from private practices, clinics, hospitals, and university health services report the number of patient visits for influenza-like illness (ILI: defined as fever and sore throat or cough) by age group and the total number of patient visits each week. These providers send specimens from patients with ILI to the state public health for viral isolation and typing. A sample of these isolates is sent to CDC for further strain characterization.

   ✓ Virologic surveillance: Many states house some of the U.S. World Health Organization collaborating laboratories that report the number of clinical specimens tested for influenza and the number of positive results by virus type and subtype. In addition, some hospital laboratories that are part of the National Respiratory and Enteric Viruses Surveillance System (NREVSS) also report the number of clinical specimens tested for influenza and the number of positive results by virus type and subtype. Additional hospital laboratories report the number of clinical specimens tested for Respiratory Synctial Virus (RSV) and the number of positive results.

✓ Surveillance for influenza and pneumonia-associated deaths: The Vital Statistics Offices in each state report the percentage of total deaths caused by influenza and pneumonia each week.

✓ Influenza-associated pediatric and adult hospitalizations: The Emerging Infections Program (EIP) monitors influenza-associated hospitalizations among children and adults in each state.

✓ Influenza-associated pediatric deaths: An influenza-associated death in a child <18 years of age is reportable in most states. Deaths are reported through a State Electronic Notifiable Disease Surveillance System (SENDSS).

✓ State influenza activity level: Each week, the state epidemiologist or designee reports influenza activity as "widespread", "regional", "local", "sporadic", or "none" based on the surveillance systems described above and additional existing bioterrorism or syndromic surveillance systems available at the time.

✓ Hospital Emergency Departments: Several hospitals transmit data (including age, sex, chief complaint) to SENDSS via secure FTP. Chief complaints are categorized into syndromes (e.g. gastrointestinal, rash, and respiratory) and analyzed using the CDC Early Aberration Reporting System (EARS).

✓ Emergency Medical Services (EMS): Data from EMS calls are collected through "First Watch," a web-based surveillance system.

✓ Schools Absenteeism: School enrollment and absenteeism data from some school districts are collected and analyzed on a weekly basis.

✓ Over-the-counter drug sales: Pharmacy data are collected through the University of Pittsburgh Real-time Outbreak and Disease Surveillance (RODS).

✓ Pneumonia surveillance: EIP conducts unexplained pneumonia surveillance, including: information on health-care workers and international travelers.

14. Surveillance Communication:

✓ Notify providers of the start of the influenza season.

✓ Send influenza report to district health offices, sentinel providers, and other interested parties (weekly during influenza season and as often as necessary after influenza season).

✓ Post updated influenza surveillance data for team.

15. State funds are sometimes used to purchase influenza vaccine.

✓ Most states maintain a Registry of Immunization Transactions and Services that includes influenza vaccine.

✓ In most states public health clinic information is posted on a statewide website, so that staff members from immunization, epidemiology, and communications can participate in monitoring the situation.

✓ Vaccine recommendations are typically posted on the public health website.

✓ Vaccine coverage estimates are derived from a Behavioral Risk Factor Surveillance System.

16. Educate public and providers on human influenza

   ✓ Fact sheet and FAQ on website and in Notifiable Disease Manual

   ✓ Influenza Outbreak Prevention and Control for Schools

   ✓ Provide media with periodic press releases

   ✓ Post surveillance data to public health website

17. Communicate with the State Department of Education

National and State Agency Decision-Making

All national and state agencies should work together to ensure that the state's preparation and response to a pandemic at all stages will be a coordinated effort within the operational principles of incident management.

References

1. CDC (2014). *School-Associated Student Homicides* – United States, 1992-2006 MMW 57 (02): 33-36

2. US Fire Administration of the US Department of Homeland Security (2014). *School School Fires* (2009-2011). Fire Report Series. Volume 14, Issue 14.

3. Cauchemez, S., Ferguson, N.M., Wachtel, C., Tegnell. A., Saor, G., Duncan, B., and Nicoll, A. (2009). *Closure of schools during an influenza pandemic.* The Lancet, Vol. 9, 1-9.

4. McGiboney, G. (2007). *Pandemic Planning for Schools.* National Federation of Urban and Suburban School Districts Conference, Charleston, West Virginia.

5. *Early Warning, Timely Response: A Guide to Safe Schools*, United States Department of Education. Retrieved 2013.

6. *The School Shooter: A Threat Assessment Perspective*, Federal Bureau of Investigation. Retrieved 2015.

7. *Crisis Management Guide*, United States Department of Defense Education. Retrieved 2014.

8. *Earthquakes and Schools.* (2008). National Clearinghouse for Educational Facilities

9. *Safe School Facilities Checklist.* (2013). National Clearinghouse for Educational Facilities.

10. *Neighborhood and Campus Facility Risk Factors.* (2009). American Clearinghouse on Educational Facilities.

11. *Multi-hazard Emergency Planning for Schools Toolkit.* (2010). Federal Emergency Management Agency.

12. *Guidelines for School Facilities.* (2000). Virginia Department of Education.

13. *Sample School Emergency Operations Plan.* (2011). Federal Emergency Management Agency.

14. *Safety and Emergency Plan.* San Francisco Unified School District.

15. Georgia Emergency Management Agency – Safe Schools Unit

16. *Emergency Management Planning for Schools.* Seattle Public School District

17. *Planning for Emergencies.* DeKalb County School District (Georgia)

18. Richards, E. P., and Rathbun, K. C. (1998). "Public Health Law." In *Maxcy-Rosenau-Last Public Health and Preventive Medicine,* ed. R. B. Wallace. Stamford, CT: Appleton and Lange.

19. *Community Emergencies.* California Contra Costa Health Services

20. *Interim Pre-Pandemic Planning Guidance.* Centers for Disease Control.
www.pandemicflu.gov

21. *Planning and Preparedness.* www.flu.gov.

22. *HHS Pandemic Influenza Plan.* United States Department of Health and Human Services.

23. *World Health Organization Checklist for Influenza Preparedness Planning.* World Health Organization.

24. *CDC Resources for Pandemic Flu.* Centers for Disease Control.

25. United States Department of Education, *Pandemic Planning*

www.ed.gov

Resources

1. Office of Safe and Drug-Free Schools Emergency Planning Web Site: Emergency planning is part of the Department's Lead and Manage My School series, a group of Web sites designed to support administrators. It offers emergency planning resources, grants, publications, and more. Accessible at http://www.ed.gov/emergencyplan

2. **Readiness and Emergency Management for Schools (REMS) Technical Assistance (TA) Center:** The REMS TA Center Web site offers additional school-based resources addressing emergency management through its four phases. Resources include three major publications series, archived training materials, referral links and the opportunity to pose direct technical assistance questions. http://rems.ed.gov

3. **Tips for Helping Students Recovering From Traumatic Events:** This brochure provides practical information for parents and students who are coping with the aftermath of a natural disaster, as well as teachers, coaches, school administrators and others who are helping those affected. Accessible at http://www.ed.gov/parents/academic/help/recovering/index.html

4. The Department of Homeland Security and the Department of Education hosted a virtual town hall on K–12 school preparedness to provide an overview of grant opportunities, planning, training and other preparedness tools available to school districts nationwide. Information is accessible at http://www.vodium.com/goto/dhs/schoolprep.asp

Appendix

SAMPLE PARENT LETTER: Prevention and Information

Use this letter to help prepare parents for a crisis such as an infectious disease before local cases are confirmed.

Dear Parents,

This letter will help your family prepare for an infectious disease that could make many people sick. It is important to know that at this time there is **no** infectious disease in our community.

However, public health officials are worried the infectious disease may change so that it can infect people and spread easily from person-to-person. This may lead to a widespread outbreak, called a pandemic.

Public health officials want people to protect themselves against an infectious disease. Here are some ways to protect your family:

- ✓ Keep children who are sick at home. Don't send them to school.
- ✓ Teach your children to wash hands with soap and water for 20 seconds. Be sure to set a good example by doing this yourself.
- ✓ Teach your children to cover coughs and sneezes with tissues or by coughing into the inside of the elbow. Be sure to set a good example by doing this yourself.
- ✓ Teach your children to stay at least three feet away from people who are sick.
- ✓ People who are sick should stay home from work or school and avoid other people until they are better.

Enclosed with this letter is a checklist to help families get ready for an infectious disease outbreak. This information can also help your family get ready for any kind of emergency.

If you have questions, please contact your school nurse, healthcare provider, or your local board of health.

The federal government website with information on planning for individuals and families: *http://www.pandemicflu.gov*
American Red Cross http://www.redcross.org
http://www.redcross.org

SAMPLE LETTER: Case in the United States

Use this letter to help prepare parents for an infectious disease after confirmation that it is spreading but is not yet in the local community.

Dear Parents,

An infectious disease is now in the United States. Health officials are concerned that it may spread to several states. This would cause a widespread outbreak, called a pandemic. So even though there are no cases nearby, we want to remind you about some ways to protect your family from getting sick:

✓ Keep children who are sick at home. Don't send them to school.

✓ Teach your children to wash hands a lot with soap and water for 20 seconds. Be sure to set a good example by doing this yourself.

✓ Teach your children to cover coughs and sneezes with tissues or by coughing into the inside of the elbow. Be sure to set a good example by doing this yourself.

✓ Teach your children to stay at least three feet away from people who are sick.

✓ People who are sick should stay home from work or school and avoid other people until they are better.

We will keep you informed if the situation changes. Please know that we are in contact with the local board of health at all times.

If you have questions, please contact your school nurse, healthcare provider, or your local board of health.

The federal government website with information on planning for individuals and families: *http://www.pandemicflu.gov*

The American Red Cross: *http://www.redcross.org*

SAMPLE LETTER TO PARENTS: Case in the State

Use this letter to give parents basic information about a pandemic outbreak and to inform parents that an infectious disease is in the state but not in your school district.

Dear Parents,

This letter will give you information about an infectious disease outbreak in [Insert county/city here]. So many people are sick that United States health officials call it a "pandemic." An infectious disease case has been confirmed in the state and in a school district. We have no confirmed or probable cases in our school district. If this changes, we will follow the CDC guidance and inform you of any changes in school operations.

At this time, the county health department tells us that students who are not ill can safely come to school. The schools will remain open. We will keep you updated with any important information.

To keep the outbreak from spreading to more people, we ask you to keep sick children home. Any children who are sick in school will be sent home. Public health officials want you to protect yourself and your family. Here are some ways to stop the spread of germs and sickness:

- ✓ Keep children who are sick at home. Don't send them to school.
- ✓ Teach your children to wash hands a lot with soap and water for 20 seconds. Be sure to set a good example by doing this yourself.
- ✓ Teach your children to cover coughs and sneezes with tissues or by coughing into the inside of the elbow. Be sure to set a good example by doing this yourself.
- ✓ Teach your children to stay away at least three feet away from people who are sick.
- ✓ People who are sick should stay home from work or school and stay away from other people until they are better.

If the infectious disease continues to spread and more students become ill, schools may close. The purpose of closing schools will be to keep children from getting sick. If schools are closed, children should stay at home and not congregate in malls or other places where large numbers of people gather. Begin planning now for childcare in your home. Recommendations may change during the course of the outbreak.

If you have questions, please contact your school nurse or healthcare provider. You can call the school hotline (INSERT NUMBER). You may also contact the local health department (INSERT NUMBER or WEBSITE).

The federal government has a website with information on planning for individuals and families: *http://www.pandemicflu.gov*, as does the American Red Cross: *http://www.redcross.org*

SAMPLE LETTER TO PARENTS and STAFF MEMBERS: Case in nearby locations *Use this letter to inform parents that an infectious disease is in nearby locations*

Dear Parents/Guardians/Staff members:

I hope you have taken time to carefully review the letter from me regarding the infectious disease that is spreading. The letter was distributed to all students and staff members and is now posted on our website. As of this writing, there have been no confirmed cases in our community or school. However, there has been a confirmed case nearby.

At this time, local public health officials tell us that students can continue to safely attend classes and schools will remain open. The outbreak will be monitored closely in the coming days and we will follow recommendations of public health in response to any changes in the status of the outbrea which could affect our schools and community.

In the event there are confirmed cases in our community or school, we will work with public health officials to carefully evaluate necessary actions. If school closings become necessary, we will make every effort to inform our school community immediately using our phone notification system, website, our education channel, and the media. Based on the circumstances, schools may be closed for days or weeks. Parents should begin now making plans for childcare in the event it is needed.

Please continue to implement the following measures to protect against the outbreak:

- ✓ Staying home from work or school and limiting contact with others when you are sick
- ✓ Covering your nose and mouth with a tissue when you cough or sneeze and properly discard used tissues. If no tissue is available, cough or sneeze into your upper sleeve, not your hands.
- ✓ Frequently washing your hands with soap and water or an alcohol-based hand sanitizer
- ✓ Avoiding touching your eyes, nose and mouth. Germs spread this way.
- ✓ Avoiding close contact with those who are ill.

Up-to-date health information can be obtained at www.cobbanddouglaspublichealth.org and www.cdc.gov/swineflu.

SAMPLE LETER TO PARENTS: *Use this letter to inform parents of school closing.*

Dear Parents,

State and local health officials have recommended that our school close immediately. This order is because of the pandemic situation and because the infectious disease is now in our community.

Our school and all other schools in our school district are immediately closed until further notice and all children should stay home. This also means that all extracurricular activities are cancelled. The school(s) may be closed for several days or weeks to reduce contact among children and stop the spread of the infectious disease. We know this is a hard time for our community and our hearts go out to those who are ill.

We will remain in contact with you to update the status of the school(s). You may wish to check our school district webpage for updated information and tune to local news stations for more information.

We know that it may be hard to get a doctor's appointment, go to a clinic or even be seen in a hospital emergency room. Here are some tips for helping those who are sick:

- ✓ Have them drink a lot of liquid (juice, water).
- ✓ Keep the sick person as comfortable as possible. Rest is important.
- ✓ For fever, sore throat and muscle aches, use ibuprofen (Motrin) or acetaminophen (Tylenol). Do not use aspirin with children or teenagers; it can cause Reye's syndrome, a life- threatening illness.
- ✓ Keep tissues and a trash bag within reach of the sick person.
- ✓ Be sure everyone in your home washes their hands frequently.
- ✓ Keep the people who are sick with the flu away from the people who are not sick.

For more information, call your healthcare provider or the local health department (insert number). We will contact you as soon as we have information about when school will reopen, and we will inform the local news media.

We encourage all parents to encourage their children to read whatever textbooks are available at home, to read other reading material at home, to practice computations and writing while at home, and (if available) access instructional programs on our website, the internet, and on public and/or access channels.

SAMPLE LETER TO PARENTS: School Re-Opens *Use this letter to inform parents schools are re-opened.*

Dear Parents,

State and local health officials have declared the pandemic outbreak is under control. Our school will open again on _____. At this time, students may safely return to school.

Even though school is opening, there are still some people who are sick. Health officials say that outbreaks sometimes happen in waves. This means more people could become sick soon again. If more people get sick, schools may need to close again. We will continue to give you any important information.

Because illnesses can be spread from person-to-person, please keep children who are sick at home. Don't send them to school.

We are looking forward to seeing your children again. Please remain alert for any news media updates and periodically check the school district's website for updates or other pertinent information.

In the near future, we will provide you more information about how school days and school work missed during the school closure will be made up. We will also send you a revised school year calendar as soon as possible.

If your child has any physical or mental health needs because of the outbreak, please let your child's school counselor know as soon as possible. If your child is too ill or weak to return to school at this time, please inform the school as soon as possible.

Sample Crisis Tabletop Exercises

The ultimate goal of a tabletop exercise is to provide school districts as well as their communities and partners an opportunity, through discussion of possible events, to better prepare for a crisis.

Set up:

Use a meeting room that will hold up to 20 people. Set aside a half day to a day for the exercise. Bring in individuals designated for leadership positions if the plans are in place or individuals that would be important in the event of a crisis, for example, a pandemic. With pandemic planning, it would be important for local health department and emergency management personnel to participate in the setup of the exercise and to participate in the tabletop exercise. Consider including non-participating observers to make notes of the exercise. Consider allowing others including local hospital administration and Red Cross to evaluate the process and provide information or answer questions as needed.

Irrespective of the present level of planning, the exercise should lead to a list of priorities for addressing an event of this type. Many of the issues that will arise will be helpful for other "all hazards" preparedness planning. All participants will be introduced to other "key partners" in the community who will also be affected by a crisis event.

It is possible to either present the entire scenario to participants or break out the particular modules and present them separately to participants as the scenario progresses. Adapt the scope and particulars as needed in relation to local circumstances. Set time limits for each module discussion.

Purpose

1. To raise awareness of issues associated with a pandemic
2. To evaluate gaps in school Crisis Management Plans

3. To begin the process of internalizing the scope and magnitude of a relatively 'worst case" crisis event

Objectives

1. Illustrate the present level of crisis planning for schools and the school district.

2. Explain how priorities are established during a crisis.

3. Illustrate the present level of interaction with all local and state agencies.

4. Describe the challenges associated with responding to a crisis event.

Setting the Crisis Scenario

1. WHO (World Health Organization) has raised the Pandemic Alert level based upon evidence of sustained and increasing levels of human-to-human transmission of an influenza virus.

2. CDC (Centers for Disease Control and Prevention) has issued travel restrictions and is encouraging public health entities to implement enhanced surveillance for patients who may have flu symptoms.

Module 1 – Setting:

1. Two weeks pass. Several patients have been laboratory confirmed to have the influenza virus that has been associated with the human-to-human transmission. These cases are initially identified on the East and West coasts of the United States.

2. CDC has issued Health Alerts to State and Local Public Health Departments urging them to take necessary public health measures to contain outbreaks.

3. Local and National media are running stories on flu cases and has increased concerns among the public.

Discussion

1. What are the issues for your schools and public health at this point in the scenario?

2. What measures does your plan call for? Do you have a plan?

3. Are your command and control systems in place (National Incident Management System based or other) to begin coordinating efforts?

4. What communications have you had with your local public health authorities?

5. How would you monitor and support your employees during this period of a pandemic?

6. Is your external communications plan functioning? How do you think the media will report the event? How will you respond to their requests for information?

7. What special or unique issues exist within schools that need to be anticipated and dealt with? (e.g. legal, technical, contractual, teachers, students, nursing, maintenance, food service)

8. Of the issues that arise, which ones would apply to other crisis management situations?

9. How did you respond upon initially hearing of cases in other parts of the country?

10. Identify which elements of crisis response infrastructure you have in place and which ones you do not. What are your strengths and weaknesses? Use this as your baseline for the rest of the scenario.

Module 2 – Setting

1. Two more weeks pass. Your state health department confirms five cases of the virus have been reported within the state.

2. Local universities and other public schools are experiencing increased absentee rates. It is not known to what degree this is a self-quarantine situation or a result of actual illness.

3. The school nurse reports indications of symptoms in the student population in your school and school district.

4. Teachers and other staff members begin calling in reporting symptoms for themselves and/or their own children or family members and cannot report to work.

5. Hospitals are reporting shortages in Personal Protective Equipment (PPE) and staff members. Once again, it is unknown how much of this is due to the virus, fear or rumor.

Discussion

1. What information do school and public health decision-makers need to know at this point?

2. How will the school district receive information from local public health?

3. How or can you obtain the information?

4. What measures would the school implement at this time?

5. How will you maintain continuity of operations during this phase?

6. Do you have a Continuity of Operations Plan (COOP) in place if the school district is closed long-term?

5. What systems/procedures do you wish you had put in place prior to this situation?

Module 3 – Setting

1. After four weeks of widespread illness and an exponentially increasing number of cases, the public is fearful of going out into the community and public health has begun implementing "voluntary" community containment measures.

2. You receive reports that some students and staff members have symptoms of the virus.

3. Local hospitals report several citizens are coming in with real or imagined virus symptoms.

4. Schools are being pressured to close by public health, but businesses, parents and others want the schools to remain open.

5. Supply systems for your schools including food and maintenance are no longer functioning.

6. People within your family are sick and others are showing symptoms. Of the 10 people initially in your decision making system, some are absent. You have not heard from and cannot contact two of them.

7. You have received an increasing number of calls from staff members who have recovered from the flu.

Discussion

1. Will schools be closed?

2. Do you have an alternative to closing schools? (i.e., screening procedure)

3. What is your criterion for closing or not closing school? Does your plan include public health in the decision to close schools?

4. If schools are closed, how and for how long? How will the announcement be made? How will employees know?

5. What are your procedures for closing schools and securing schools?

6. What are your plans for educational continuity?

Summary

1. Acknowledge that this scenario represents a "worst case" scenario and decide if future exercises (after improvement actions are taken) should function at this or a "better case" level based upon existing planning estimates. This tabletop example is primarily to provide a baseline for planning purposes.

✓ Discuss how well your local community response plans are coordinated.

✓ Explain how you would prioritize needs at various points during the event (modules).

✓ What role would, should or could the school and/or school system play within the local response to the event?

2. Describe logistical challenges associated with a pandemic flu event.

3. Knowing that there will likely be a second wave of the pandemic influenza coming, how will you prepare for that? What will be different? What will be the same in that event?

4. Provide an anonymous process evaluation form for participants and technical assistance providers to submit.

Additional Sample Questions to Guide a Tabletop Exercise for Pandemic Planning

1. What kind of educational material is available to faculty, staff members, students and parents about pandemic influenza?

2. Does the plan outline the decision-making process, key personnel, and criteria for cancelling classes or closing schools? For example, are decisions made by the education or health agency? At the state or local level? Or, collaboratively?

3. Have faculty, staff members, community and emergency response partners been involved in providing input and feedback for crisis planning for schools?

4. Is the school district's current emergency response plan suited for a pandemic influenza outbreak?

5. Is there a communication plan for keeping schools informed of decisions regarding school scheduling and closures?

6. Does the school system have a surveillance system for absences? If so, is this system linked to the local health department or other health-related entity?

7. Does the school plan adequately address the maintenance of educational operations in the case of pandemic? If so, what plan is in place for maintaining continuity of instruction (tele-schooling, individual/group mentoring) for students?

8. What is the school procedure for school closure when a public health emergency has been declared?

9. To address the fear of a pandemic influenza outbreak, does the school district have the capabilities to provide psychological support for student and faculty/staff members when needed?

10. Does the school have established communication protocols with parents, staff members, community and emergency response partners, such as local health departments and media, before and during a public health emergency?

11. What is the school's plan to communicate with media for latest information dissemination?

12. What is the school's plan to communicate with public health during pandemic influenza outbreak?

13. What key procedures are in place to support the continuity of essential school operations, during a long term school closure? The following items should be considered during discussion

    ✓ Air quality/HVAC system functions

    ✓ Decontamination

✓ Safe learning environment and alternative teaching and learning methods

✓ Payroll

✓ Line of Succession for all key staff members

14. How much time/school days does the district need to prepare to reopen individual schools within the district? For example, how many days are needed to:

✓ Replenish cleaning and hygiene supplies;

✓ Assess, identify and prioritize the order of individual schools to reopen;

✓ Assess staff members capacity, including substitutes (remember, nearby school district will also be recruiting substitutes);

✓ Inform and train staff members on health and prevention issues;

✓ Inform parents of school reopening plans and procedures; and

✓ Inform, train and modify learning environment to meet the needs of available staff members and healthy students at school alongside alternative strategies addressing those at home.

15. What is the school's plan to provide psychological support to faculty, staff members, students and parents who have been in isolation for three months and are having difficulty re-adjusting to "regular life?"

16. What is the school's plan to maintain monitoring for possible resurgence of the virus?

17. Does the emergency management plan provide protocols standards for decontaminating the schools and standards providing for a safe and healthy environment?

18. What kind of resources does a district need in order to rehabilitate the learning environment (i.e., what supplies and tool, how many staff members, how many days.) For example, if the school was used as a community facility, such as a makeshift hospital or clinic or vaccine distribution site, what are the procedures for sanitizing the facilities?

19. Does the district have agreements in place with local and/or State emergency response entities regarding decontamination processes and determinations of safety?

20. Does the plan provide criteria for students and staff members re-entering the school community and recontamination prevention programs? For example, those who have been exposed in the last seven days are not permitted to attend school. For those attending school, are there sufficient hand-washing supplies and information awareness campaigns preventing the spread of germs?

21. What are the school's procedures to maintain communication with parents, staff members, community and public health in case the virus resurfaces?

22. What is the school's plan to provide psychological support for faculty, staff members, and students due to influenza related serious illnesses or fatalities?

23. Does the school plan adequately address key issues, such as school faculty and staff members training in pandemic flu knowledge and handling high morbidity and/or mortality in schools, in dealing with a mass influenza outbreak?

24. What issues did you identify in your procedures that could hinder pan flu efforts?

25. Does the school and district emergency response plan adequately address key issues faced during a long-term school closure, including continuity of instruction, feasibility of feeding students in school meal programs, continuity of business operations (e.g., payroll) and leave policies for teachers?

26. Do the school procedures properly coordinate communication response activity among schools, community and public health during a pandemic influenza event? In your opinion, what can be done to maintain and coordinate communication during an emergency situation such as the pandemic influenza scenario presented in the exercise?

27. Does the plan discuss/include resources to the district and schools?

28. What are the roles and responsibilities of parents throughout the district's pandemic influenza plan? Do they participate in prevention-mitigation activities? Preparedness? Response? Recovery? Are parents involved in the decision to cancel classes? At what level are they engaged?

29. Overall, is the school capable of effectively and efficiently recovering from a mass influenza outbreak in order to resume a safe learning environment? Can the team identify methods for hastening the disinfectant process? What social distancing strategies can be added?

Crisis Readiness for School Nutrition Programs

Before a crisis occurs

1. Maintain, and update frequently, a list of all staff members with home addresses, e-mail addresses, phone numbers and crisis contact information.

2. Maintain a written record of all persons who have keys and access to kitchen and cafeteria entrances, walk-in coolers/freezers and dry storage areas.

3. Determine if vendors have a crisis plan for continuity or recovery of supply deliveries when a crisis occurs that reduces the workforce. If they do not have a plan, encourage them to do so.

4. In the event of an infectious disease crisis focus on prevention as the most important measure in stopping anyone from contracting an infectious disease. Hand-washing is the number one preventive measure. Preparation in schools for an infectious disease should include the provision of proper supplies in restrooms and teaching students the importance of hand-washing at all grade levels. Students should also be taught the importance of coughing and sneezing into their upper sleeve to avoid spreading infectious diseases. These measures are important for anyone in a school, but are even more important for those preparing meals in school cafeterias. Good personal hygiene will help prevent the transfer of infectious diseases from hand to mouth as food is consumed.

5. Be aware of the symptoms to look for during infectious disease events. The Centers for Disease Control and Prevention defines infectious type disease illnesses as having the following symptoms: A fever of 101.5°F or higher and one of the following – cough, sore throat, headache and/or muscle ache, nausea, vomiting and diarrhea

may accompany the above symptoms. Any food service worker with these symptoms needs to be sent home immediately and the food service area cleaned.

6. Once an infectious disease spreads, schools may begin to see a gradual increase in absenteeism. At some point, predetermined by the school's Crisis Management Plan, parents should be notified of the increased student absenteeism and what symptoms to look for in their children – which should also encourage parents to keep sick children at home. When this occurs, there will probably be an immediate further increase in absenteeism. This alone will decrease the number of meals that need to be prepared. A daily update on student attendance will help the school nutrition manager estimate the amount of food preparation needed for each day.

7. Once an infectious disease becomes widespread in several states it is likely that it will spread to schools and sometimes the spread can move quickly. With that in mind, some preparations need to be done in advance, such as:

   a. Vendors may have to close due to staff members shortages. A list of back-up vendors and contact information should be updated regularly.

   b. Maintain at least a five-day supply of food products. These foods should include at least a two-day supply of products that can be easily served in bag lunches. A regular five-day supply will probably be enough for more than five days because of student absenteeism.

   c. Carefully maintain proper cleaning and sanitizing procedures and perform routine maintenance on equipment. Proper cleaning and sanitizing is always necessary, but it takes on increased importance when there is an infectious disease outbreak. Dishwashing machines must be maintained to operate according to the data plate on the front of the machine.

d.   There may be staff member shortages in school nutrition. Plan to limit menu items and possibly provide bag lunches if necessary or if it will make the workload easier. Maintain enough disposable plates, cups and utensils for five days use in case staff members shortages make it difficult to operate the dish and utensil cleaning machines.

e.   Update employee health guidelines to reflect the necessity for excluding employees from the facility should symptoms of sore throat with fever, vomiting and/or diarrhea occur. In addition, a required condition for reinstatement during a infectious disease event must be written documentation from a health practitioner that the person is healthy to return to work.

f.   Prevention is of primary importance therefore hand washing takes on increased significance. There are no hand sinks available in most school cafeteria dining areas. The second choice for hand sanitizing is hand sanitizer. Maintain a supply of hand sanitizer that will be enough for treating the average number of students coming to a cafeteria for five days.

g.   The most effective sanitizer for killing viruses is chlorine bleach. Maintain a supply of chlorine bleach for sanitizing cafeteria tables, seats, door knobs and other surfaces (1/4 cup bleach to 1 gallon water). Note that school nutrition only purchases chlorine bleach and other supplies for use by school nutrition. Replace chlorine bleach with new product at least once each year as the strength may weaken over time. If the school does not want to use chlorine bleach, an EPA-registered hospital disinfectant or a sanitizer that is EPA-registered and labeled for activity against bacteria and viruses may be substituted. Use the disinfectant or sanitizer according to the manufacturer's instructions.

h. Train all staff members to be aware of infectious disease symptoms and their roles in the Crisis Management Plan.

8. If delivery of milk becomes a problem, contact the state school nutrition program for alternate solutions, or contact USDA.

9. Self-service salad bars and buffets should be discontinued during an infectious disease outbreak. Viruses do not multiply in food, but it only takes a very small number to make someone ill. If a student who is ill coughs or rubs his nose and then touches food or contaminates the food in another way, the next person to choose the same food item could be infected.

10. At some point students who are showing no symptoms may be prevented from eating in the school cafeteria in order to control the spread of infectious diseases. Bag lunches will probably be the best solution to feeding these students. Sanitize the cart that is used to transport the bag lunches to each classroom with a chlorine bleach solution, at least daily (1/4 cup chlorine bleach per gallon of water), and allow to air dry (another product may be used as stated in 7. g. above if chlorine bleach is not purchased). Provide large garbage cans outside the occupied classrooms according to number of

children and amount of waste materials. Custodians should tie up garbage bags promptly and dispose of them as soon as possible after the meal period.

11. Custodians should be provided with chlorine bleach by the school administrator or maintenance department to sanitize desks, classroom doorknobs and handrails daily and properly sanitize an area should vomiting occur. If the cafeteria and/or other floor areas are carpeted, a steam cleaner is the best alternative to using chlorine bleach. If chlorine bleach is not preferred for sanitizing surfaces such as desktops and doorknobs due to the possibility of staining carpets, an EPA-registered hospital disinfectant or other EPA-registered sanitizer labeled for activity against bacteria and viruses may be substituted.

While a school is closed

1. Once the absenteeism rate reaches a certain point predetermined by a school's Crisis Management Plan and/or by the local health authority, a school may need to be closed. Maintain contact with school administration to know the status of the situation and when the school will be reopened.

2. There may be a need for outside feeding programs similar to seamless summer nutrition programs if the school, in agreement with local emergency authorities, thinks it is appropriate. If a school is not already approved for a seamless summer nutrition program, contact USDA for approval. If any of the guidelines need to be altered due to the situation, contact the USDA for a waiver.

3. Many schools have the proper insulated equipment to transport foods, especially if they have summer programs or a cater food. If a school doesn't have the necessary equipment to maintain proper

temperatures, the equipment can possibly be borrowed from local caterers or non-potentially hazardous foods can be provided in bag lunches. Note that local caterers will probably have reduced business during a time of an infectious disease spread since one of the recommendations to the public is to stay home and not participate in large gatherings.

4. If outside feeding is not needed or there are not enough staff members to operate such a program and it appears that the school will be closed for more than a week, discard refrigerated foods that have been prepared on-site or commercially prepared and opened. In lieu of discarding, you may consider wrapping the food products securely, dating them properly and freezing. Fresh produce and milk should never be frozen. Discard any food that has a sell-by/use-by/expiration date within the projected length of closure time period. Always inventory and record types and amounts of food products that are discarded on production records so that costs are reflected USDA reports. Contact vendors to suspend deliveries until further notice.

5. Depending on circumstances and staff member availability, continue daily monitoring temperatures of refrigerated equipment. Keep in mind that personal safety and protection are most important. Do not worry about monitoring equipment if instructions have been given not to return to the school premises or for everyone to stay at home.

6. In the event that a school has an immediate closing with only one day or less notification, do as much as possible to secure food products. It is recommended that managers take contact information with them so that any necessary phone calls to vendors and others can be done from another location.

Re-opening a school

1. Contact all employees to find out their health status and availability to come back to work.

2. Contact all vendors to notify them of time and date the school plans to re-open and to find out when they can make deliveries.

3. All food contact surfaces should be cleaned and sanitized unless they were completely wrapped with plastic wrap or other secure material to prevent contamination.

4. Check all food products and discard when any of the following is found:

    a. Signs of being out of temperature (excess ice crystals are a sign of refreezing, unusual odors and coloration).

    b. Signs of vandalism and tampering.

    c. Food products have expired use-by/sell-by/expiration dates.

5. In the event of vandalism or tampering with food products or any area of the school kitchen and cafeteria, notify the school principal and the police.

6. If the school has been closed for more than two weeks and/or there is any evidence of food temperature abuse, vandalism, facility damage or pest infestation, contact the local health department to assist in evaluation of food products and other food safety/sanitation concerns.

Acknowledgements

The author would like to thank the following for their contributions to the book in many ways, including information and inspiration: Marilyn Watson, Jeff Hodges, Howard Hendley, Lou Erste, Quentin Fretwell, Charley English, Charlie Dawson, and Dr. Patrick O'Neal.

A special acknowledgement goes to Dr. Robert Freeman and Dr. Edward Bouie, Sr. for their steadfast and lasting influence on the author's ongoing efforts to live up to their fine example of servant leadership.

The book Crisis Management Planning in Schools is a valuable addition to the body of work necessary for schools to be fully prepared to handle crises situations. -Charley English, Deputy Director of Emergency Management

Dr. McGiboney is a recognized expert on school safety and management, and his work is a valuable resource for schools at all levels. -Dr. Ron Stephens, Director, National School Safety Center

This book was written to support and encourage the development and implementation of a comprehensive crisis management and prevention plan in schools and school districts. It contains protocols and procedures for a wide variety of crisis situations, including a comprehensive section on pandemic and epidemic planning and response. It is designed to be used as a general resource and as a training tool. It contains specific information, protocols aimed at operational functions, and it can be adapted to any type of school setting, including non-traditional school settings. In addition to being a crisis planning guide and training manual, the book is intended to be a quick reference resource, which makes the numerous checklists and specific language valuable as an immediate aid.

Garry W. McGiboney, Ph.D.
Dr. McGiboney is a nationally recognized expert on school leadership, school crisis management, and crisis planning and response. He has made hundreds of presentations across the United States and is often a keynote speaker at state and national conferences, including presentations for the United States Department of Education, United States Department of Justice, United States Office of Special Education Program, and others. He has published over 30 professional articles and is the author of three books. Dr. McGiboney has appeared on CNN, A&E, Discovery Channel, Public Broadcasting Service, National Public Radio, Nickelodeon Network and many local and regional television and radio programs. He has been quoted in Time Magazine, Education Week, USA Today, and many others, including the international press. Dr. McGiboney is the recipient of numerous awards, such as the NAACP Educator of the Year, National Association of School Psychologists Friend of Children Award, University System of Georgia Hall of Fame for Services to Children, and others. He has a Ph.D. from Georgia State University in psychology and administration.

EPC -
EINSTAR PUBLISHING COMPANY
MIAMI AND NEW YORK

Made in the USA
Columbia, SC
31 May 2018